Stop and Make Money

Founded in 1807, John Wiley & Sons is the oldest independent publishing company in the United States. With offices in North America, Europe, Australia, and Asia, Wiley is globally committed to developing and marketing print and electronic products and services for our customers' professional and personal knowledge and understanding.

The Wiley Trading series features books by traders who have survived the market's ever changing temperament and have prospered—some by reinventing systems, others by getting back to basics. Whether a novice trader, professional, or somewhere in-between, these books will provide the advice and strategies needed to prosper today and well into the future.

For a list of available titles, please visit our Web site at www.WileyFinance.com.

Stop and Make Money

How to Profit in the Stock Market
Using Volume and Stop Orders

RICHARD W. ARMS, JR.

BICENTENNIAL
1807
WILEY
2007
BICENTENNIAL

John Wiley & Sons, Inc.

Published by John Wiley & Sons, Inc., Hoboken, New Jersey.
Published simultaneously in Canada.

Wiley Bicentennial Logo: Richard J. Pacifico

For general information on our other products and services or for technical support, please contact our Customer Care Department within the United States at (800) 762-2974, outside the United States at (317) 572-3993 or fax (317) 572-4002.

Designations used by companies to distinguish their products are often claimed as trademarks. In all instances where John Wiley & Sons, Inc. is aware of a claim, the product names appear in initial capital or all capital letters. Readers, however, should contact the appropriate companies for more complete information regarding trademarks and registration.

Wiley also publishes its books in a variety of electronic formats. Some content that appears in print may not be available in electronic formats. For more information about Wiley products, visit our Web site at www.wiley.com.

MetaStock charts courtesy of Equis International, a Reuters company. All rights reserved.

Library of Congress Cataloging-in-Publication Data:

Arms, Richard W., 1935–
    Stop and make money : how to profit in the stock market using volume and stop orders / Richard W. Arms, Jr.
        p. cm. – (Wiley trading series)
    Includes index.
    ISBN 978-0-470-12996-8 (cloth/cd-rom)
  1. Stocks–Charts, diagrams, etc.   2. Stock price forecasting.   3. Investment analysis.   I. Title.
    HG4916.A715 2008
    332.63′2042–dc22

                                                                                        2007025163

Printed in the United States of America.

10 9 8 7 6 5 4 3 2 1

For June: wife, companion, and best friend for half a century, so far.

Contents

Acknowledgments

My thanks to Betty Annis, who spent many hours reading the manuscript and detecting my prolific errors. Thanks to Paul Butt, for his long and detailed memories of how the markets used to be, way back when we were rookie brokers. Charlie Kirkpatrick, author and expert on technical analysis, was extremely helpful in listening to my ideas and lending professional expertise. Stock search methods and ideas were greatly assisted by Charles Brauer and his superb ability to create unique computer programs. My thanks to my editors, Kevin Commins and Emilie Herman at John Wiley & Sons, for the many ideas and subsequent debates over titles and format. But foremost is my appreciation for the understanding of my friends and family, and especially June, for tiptoeing past my office door as I put this book together.

About the Author

Richard W. Arms, Jr. is one of the world's most respected stock market personalities. Since 1996, he has been advising a select group of money managers and financial institutions in the United States, Europe, and Canada. In addition, he writes a twice-weekly Internet column for *RealMoney*, the institutional service from TheStreet.com.

Mr. Arms invented and then popularized the Arms Index. This indicator, often called TRIN, has become a mainstay of market analysis. It appears daily in the *Wall Street Journal* and weekly in *Barron's*. His index crosses the CNBC tape as "ARMS" every few minutes throughout every trading day. He developed Equivolume charting, which has become a popular method featured on MetaStock and many other technical software packages. He is the inventor of Ease of Movement, volume cyclicality, and volume-adjusted moving averages.

His books (*Profits in Volume*, *Volume Cycles in the Stock Market*, *The Arms Index*, and *Trading without Fear*) have been translated into a number of languages, and his methodology is familiar to most stock market traders and professionals in every financial center. He was the 1995 recipient of the Market Technicians Association Outstanding Contribution Award for his lifetime contribution to technical analysis.

The Great Opportunity

In the pages that follow we are going to look at a cohesive gathering of tools that can make you money. It is a technical approach to the market, which has only one objective: buying cheaper than you sell. One of the primary tools will be the stop order, hence the title of this book. But that is just a part of the entire technique of trading, which is based on a proper recognition of the importance volume plays in the marketplace. It is a story about trading, not long-term investing.

Never before in history have conditions been more conducive to stock market trading! All the various impediments that traders faced in the past have been either eliminated or reduced to extremely low levels. This has been due to two factors. The first is the development of a free and competitive market, with ever-lower commission rates. The second factor is the immense leaps in technology that have so radically changed the marketplace. These two factors, in combination, have leveled the playing field to the extent that the trader in rural New Mexico has every advantage that the trader on Wall Street has.

By trading I mean taking advantage of the shorter-term stock market moves. The actual time frame to be used is addressed in Chapter 7. The primary concern is with buying a stock (or selling it short) in order to gain price movement, with little regard for the fundamental factors involved in the underlying stock that is being used as the vehicle for achieving those gains. In the past, trading has had a number of built-in drawbacks that have made it far more difficult to be successful. Now those drawbacks have been largely eliminated. That does not mean that it is easy to trade successfully. It still takes knowledge, ability, objectivity, and hard work. But the opportunity is the best it has ever been.

Imagine, if you will, what it was like when I first became a retail stockbroker, more years ago than I like to contemplate. I started off with a small independent company that cleared through a larger member firm. We were far from New York, and everything was done by Teletype. If a customer wanted to buy, say, 100 shares of DuPont, the first step was to wire the office we cleared through for a quote. Some minutes later a quote and market size would print out on our Teletype machine as a thin band of gum-backed paper clicking out of the machine. Next the client would decide what he wanted to do, whereupon another message would be typed into the machine, with the particulars of the client's order to buy the stock, at a price or a limit. If it were a market order, the report might come in some minutes later. Of course, some offices had tickers, so that prices could be read as they came across on the ticker tape, giving a bit more timely information. But it was still a very slow and difficult way of trading. Time lags meant poor information and uncertain executions.

The client would pay a commission that averaged about $38 on such a trade. It could not be less than a formula-derived commission, agreed upon, and abided by, by all exchange members. If the client was buying 1,000 shares, the rate was 10 times the 100-share rate. There were no break points for larger orders; it was always a multiple of the 100-share rate. It was illegal to negotiate a lower commission rate. Of course, it made trading very expensive. A stock would have to move a long distance, often nearly a point, in order to get to breakeven before making money. The brokerage firm made money, the broker made money, and with a little bit of luck maybe even the customer was able to show a profit after absorbing commissions, transfer fees, and even a penalty if the trade was an odd lot. But it was a big hit for the trader to absorb.

Negotiated commission rates have now been around for many years, and ever since the change was allowed, commissions have come down and down. The competitiveness of the marketplace, combined with the efficiency of modern technology, has made it possible for traders to go in and out of stocks for such low rates that they are almost negligible. Commissions alone should never again be a reason for not making a trade. Rates for online trades are being offered to traders by many different online brokers for well under $10 per trade. It is no longer a function of, or a multiple of, the number of shares being traded. A hundred shares or 5,000 shares; the commission is the same. That means that a trade is often done at a fraction of a penny per share. So a stock only has to move a few cents to be a worthwhile transaction from the standpoint of the trader. This is a huge plus. The small trader is no longer placed at a disadvantage.

The biggest and best thing to happen to trading in many years, though, has been online trading. It has opened the door for trading in ways that have never been possible before. Analysts, sitting in their homes in front of their computers, can place orders directly and get immediate executions and reports on those transactions. The time delay, especially with market orders or with very liquid stocks, is often so short that the transaction is, for all intents, instantaneous. The power of computers and the Internet has eliminated the distance from Main Street to Wall Street. Decisions can be made and trades executed from a hotel room, from a coffee shop, from an airport, from almost anywhere. In the battle to become dominant, brokerages have provided more and more information and better and better access, at lower and lower prices. It is the trader who has benefited the most. It also has meant that traders can place orders of any sort, near the market or away from the market, with time limits or not, and not be burdening a busy person behind a desk with having to tend to all these orders. In the strategies we will be looking at this is very important.

Of course, the benefits of online trading can be looked upon as a detriment, too. So much information and such easy trading can lead to doing too much trading. But there are ways to get around that problem. The methods we will be discussing are designed to avoid that very real pitfall.

The greatest benefit derived from the advent of online trading has been a psychological one: anonymity—not the desire to remain anonymous, but the ability to not have to justify actions. It is far easier to place an order if there is no requirement to tell someone what you are doing. It also leads to much less inhibited and much more systematic trading. Going into a brokerage house, or picking up a phone and talking to a broker, places the trader in a position wherein it is necessary to explain why a certain action is being taken. You never want to be in that position! It is for this same reason that I always make it a point to never discuss my trades with anyone. It may make you sound important at a party to talk of your stock market successes, but if you do so you have put yourself in the position of justifying your actions to someone else. If you mention a stock you like, both you and the person you spoke to will remember that conversation. My concern is not with people who might act on what they think is a hot tip (they should know better), but with the effect it can have on my own judgment. I know I may see that individual on the golf course in a week or two and be asked if I still own the stock, if it made money, and so forth. Just by speaking of the stock I have changed my own emotional involvement. I have put myself into the position of proving how smart I am. Trading through a live person is similar. It removes the objectivity of the method and inserts a need to look good. Therefore, I suggest that any serious trader use an automated order entry system. It is never necessary to explain yourself to a computer.

The third reason we are in the best of times is the availability of data. I do not mean stock tips, rumors, research reports, or television gurus. They are certainly more available than ever before also, and need to be guarded against. But the electronic availability of instantaneous prices, ranges, volume, bids and asks, with market sizes, market indicators, and market statistics, is another way in which the playing field has been flattened. A great deal of that information is available through your online broker, or you may want to subscribe to a real-time data feed.

And no advantage is more apparent than that of personal account information. Do you want to know what open orders you have? No need to check lists on your desk; just click on the online broker's page for your account that shows your current orders. Do you want to know your buying power? It's right there. You can check on a stock and see how much profit or loss you have—and not as of yesterday's close but as of the last trade, perhaps seconds ago. Want to see what trades you have done in the past week, or the past month? Just ask the computer. At the end of the year the broker even gives you a rundown on the whole year for your taxes.

Put all of this together with the extremely sophisticated software and data that will supply you with charts, and you have everything you are going to need. In my first book, *Profits in Volume* (Marketplace Books, 1971), in which I put forth the idea of Equivolume charting, all the illustrations were hand drawn. Every chart had been meticulously constructed, not for the book, but for my own trading and advising functions. It was some years later that the software was created that drew Equivolume charts. Now the software is available to do charts of every time frame and scaling option. They can be tied to a data flow so that they are real-time or end-of-day charts. When a stock did split or change radically in volume or activity characteristics, I used to throw away the chart and start a new one with a different scale. Now the computer makes the adjustment. Where I could follow, at best, a few dozen stocks, today the data covers many thousands of issues. It means that the trader now has the problem opposite to mine. I couldn't look at enough situations. Now there are so many possible trades out there that it is difficult to whittle down the candidates. But there are also ways of asking a computer to do that whittling.

So, with this level playing field we have what I like to call an uninhibiting marketplace. All the factors that once inhibited the sort of trading we will be talking about in the pages that follow have been removed or reduced to a level where they are no longer a problem.

- Commissions were once an inhibition, forcing us to say that we would hold a position because we had already paid a commission to get in, and it would cost another commission to get out. Now they are so low as to no longer be a valid excuse for inaction.
- Pride was once an inhibition, but now no one but you and your computer need to know what you are doing.
- Record keeping was once an inhibition. Now it is all done for you.
- Lack of information was once a deterrent. Now, if there is a problem, it is that the information is so pervasive as to bring on confusion.
- Extremely sophisticated charting software is now at your fingertips.
- Slowness of executions and lack of instant communications made trading difficult in the past. Not any longer.
- Geography no longer places you at a disadvantage.
- Size of trades is not a factor anymore.

One of the most important parts of the methodology that follows is the use of stop orders. There was a time when they were considered a nuisance by your broker. Now you can place all the orders you want and never feel the need to justify your actions. And that is very important, because, as you will read, you should place a great many more stop orders than ever get executed. You will see that the stop order, whether to get into a position or out of a position, is your best friend. The ability to effectively use stop orders has been greatly enhanced by the leveling of the playing field.

I once had a co-worker who used to tell me, "Dick, you are standing in the middle of your own acre of diamonds." If he was right at that time, we must now all be standing in the middle of our own square mile of diamonds. Never before have the conditions been as good for traders as they are now. In the pages that follow we are going to see ways that will help in picking up some of those diamonds.

Let's Get Started

B efore we get to all the details, we are going to look at a couple of trades in the first two chapters. From them you will get a good idea where we are heading, and how we are going to get there. You may even be ready to get your feet wet with some actual trading. Later you will be able to fill in the details, but it is necessary to first get a feel for the overall methodology.

HOW THE BEGINNING OF THE BOOK IS STRUCTURED

Chapter 1 offers an example of a buy; Chapter 2 analyzes a short sale. You are not going to understand all of the intricacies of the trades unless you are already thoroughly familiar with the methodology. With that in mind, what I have done is insert, just in these two chapters, references to other chapters.

This is how the references look in Chapters 1 and 2.

Please read through these two chapters *at least* once without going to the other referenced chapters. Then, if you want, you can browse through the chapters or you can read them in order. Some later chapters are not referenced at all in these first chapters, although they do contain important information (particularly the chapters on forecasting market direction, since market direction can have a very big effect on trading results). Investment decisions are affected by the direction of the overall market, so be sure that you go to those chapters at some point.

Computer manufacturers have found that the buyers almost never have the patience to read through an owner's manual before hooking up, plugging in, turning on the computer, and stumbling around without knowing what they are doing. The manufacturers have therefore inserted quick-start guides. These one or two pages are enough to keep new computer owners from getting into too much trouble. Later the users are likely to go to the owner's manual and fill in the gaps in their knowledge. These two chapters are the quick-start guide for successful trading using the Equivolume methodology and the trading techniques that go with it. If you just can't stand to wait and want to fire up the charting program, follow the examples in these two chapters, and start to trade, this quick-start guide will probably keep you out of deep trouble. Then, if you run into problems or questions, you can go to the referenced chapters to get more information. But the rest of the book is the owner's manual. If you want to do it right, you are going to need to eventually read it all.

Chapters 20 to 23 deal with determining market direction.

A WINNING TRADE

What a great trade! You did everything right. You bought the stock just before the move got going, you held it through the entire advance, and then you sold it right near the top. All the way up you were protected by a stop order so you didn't have to lie awake worrying about the position. You didn't let greed get the best of you, so you didn't sell after the initial advance; you waited for the move to run its course. You had an objective, and it worked. It took six months, but the stock moved from 24 to 37. That's 54 percent in six months. If you could do that twice a year and you let the profits build, you would turn each $10,000 you started with into over $23,700 in the first year. In 10 years, at that rate, your $10,000 would grow to over $56 million!

It's a great feeling, and it sometimes happens. But often it doesn't go quite that way. Often you get out with a loss. Sometimes you take a small profit and leave a big one on the table. Occasionally you change your mind and get out because of a news item. But more often you decline to take a position in the first place because of the news background. There are times when you would have bought the stock, but the market seemed too risky. There are other times when you moved in too soon, thinking the stock just couldn't go any lower. There are times when you bought too late, because you didn't want to take too much risk.

In other words, a great trade does not happen often enough, and when it does, a great deal of the reason for your success may be just luck. In the pages that follow, you will be finding out why some of your trades worked so well and putting rules to your trading that you will make the big successes more frequent, and the losses smaller and less frequent.

To do this we will first pull apart and inspect each move in an ideal success story. We will try to put rules to the trading that will tend to capitalize upon the things that work. We will try to find the pitfalls that need to be avoided.

GENERAL MOTORS IN 2006

First, let's look at the success story alluded to earlier. In the early months of 2006 General Motors appeared to be the most hated stock on Wall Street. No one had anything good to say about it. The company was having massive troubles. The news media were full of negative stories about the company. You had to be either insane or a technician to buy the stock, or so it seemed. But there was obviously some buying that was going on, and any technician would have had to be aware of it. Evidently, in spite of the news, someone was accumulating the stock in a big way.

For information on how to use and not use the news, see Chapter 3. For reasons for using technical analysis, also see Chapter 3.

In early May, at the last entry on the chart shown in Figure 1.1, General Motors had been in a sideways move for about six months. After making a low in late December of 2005 it held well, making numerous attempts to rally but being repeatedly turned back. But the point is that it was not going lower in spite of the negative press and the gloom on

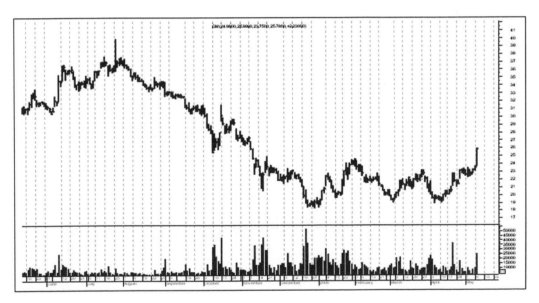

FIGURE 1.1 Bar Chart of General Motors.

the street. The reason it was not going lower was simply that there were buyers willing to soak up all offered stock when the price got down around the $19 level. But there were also aggressive sellers willing to lose stock any time the price got up around $24 or $25. The buyers did not yet have the upper hand, but neither did the sellers, hence the six-month period of consolidation.

Figure 1.1 is a bar chart. Each vertical line represents one day of trading. The top of each posting is the high of the day, and the bottom is the low of the day. The price scale is shown on the right-hand side of the chart, and is an arithmetic scale in this case. Volume is shown as a histogram across the bottom of the chart. This is the traditional way of graphing stock action, and it is useful and effective. But we will henceforth be looking at and using a method I believe is more informative. It is called Equivolume charting.

To learn about the construction of Equivolume charts, read Chapter 5.

Figure 1.2 is an Equivolume chart. It looks at General Motors over the same time frame as the bar chart shown first. In this methodology, the volume has been brought up off the lower margin and been included in the price plot. Therefore, each day is represented as a box. The high and low are the same as the high and the low on the bar chart, but the width of the box indicates the volume. The wider the box, the heavier the volume. It also means that the shape of the box is an accurate picture of the balance of fear and greed in the stock on that day. We are not seeing any new information. We are

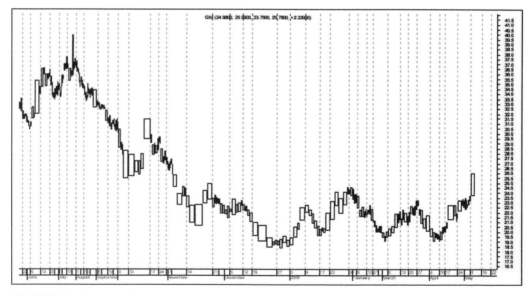

FIGURE 1.2 Equivolume Chart of General Motors.

just looking at the same information in a different way. By including the volume in the price plot we are getting a different picture of the data, and one that is more informative.

Now we have a different picture of that consolidation area we noticed on the bar chart.

Chapters 8 and 13 to 18 cover the interpretation of Equivolume charts.

The most important thing that immediately comes to our attention, or should, is the width of the various Equivolume entries. We are able to immediately ascertain where the volume is occurring. Notice that the wide boxes were mostly on the down days in the months leading up to the end of the year. Heavy volume on the down days indicated the stock was under distribution. But then something seemed to change. In early January, and on every rally thereafter, volume expanded, and on every pullback volume tended to decrease. The serious investors in the marketplace had inadvertently tipped their hand, and we saw, by looking at the volume, the strategy of their game. They were moving in and buying the stock until they drove it to the top of the range, and then they backed away and waited for another opportunity. The pullbacks were on lighter volume, because the big buyers had gone to the sidelines.

At the time of the last entry on this chart, though, there has been another change. The top of the consolidation, the six months of directionless trading, has been decisively penetrated. We have what I like to call a power box.

See Chapter 8 to learn about power boxes.

Both volume and trading range have become larger as the level of resistance has been broken. That resistance is the top of the consolidation area we have been watching. It is the level at which the buyers have moved to the sidelines in previous rallies. Now, though, the buyers have kept on going and have broken the stock out of the consolidation. It is an unequivocal sign of strength.

Chapter 16 illustrates support and resistance levels.

Looking more closely, there is much more information to be gleaned from Figure 1.3, which shows a number of trend lines, support and resistance levels, and volume signals. Had we been watching this stock back at the first of the year, we would have been aware of the first sign of strength. It was enough to break the descending trend line and suggest a change of direction. Volume was heavier, and the stock even left a small gap behind as it moved away from the very narrow base formed in the waning days of the prior year.

Gaps are explained in Chapter 13.

One might have decided at that point to buy the stock. The problem, though, was the very narrow base. If the market could be thought of as controlled by causes and effects, the narrow base provided very little cause, so we could not anticipate a very large effect.

FIGURE 1.3 Annotated Equivolume Chart.

In other words, it looked as though a move upward would be small and brief. Of course, if our intention was to trade each small move, we might have been inclined to move in on the stock.

Chapter 7 helps in ascertaining what wave pattern to trade.

But assuming we had already decided we were looking for the more lasting moves, the narrowness of the base would have kept us on the sidelines. Even the second move up on volume would have been met with skepticism, in that it did nothing more than fulfill the objective implied by that narrow base. The width of a base often indicates how far a move will go.

Price objectives and their measurement are covered in Chapter 18.

As the various swings built the wider base, we could see that some very regular support and resistance levels were being established. It is interesting to note that the first rally established a level of resistance that was visited again later. Then it held the stock back again for a few days before the power box that has become our focus. This important level is marked as the lower of the two resistance lines. The pullbacks also established a zone of support, so we ended up with a very well defined trading zone. A breakout through the top of that zone would suggest that it was a zone of accumulation, and a cause for a more lasting effect.

Chapter 18 provides a discussion of accumulation and distribution.

Now it looked as though it was time to buy the stock. But wait, we know that most of the time a breakout is followed by a pullback before the move really gets going. Do we want to jump in at this price, or do we want to try to buy it at a better price after a pullback? Perhaps the best way is to watch for the pullback, and buy just as soon as the advance resumes. A buy stop order can accomplish that.

Chapter 10 explains using a stop order to get into a position.

THE MECHANICS OF BUYING

The next question needs to be: How many shares? Also, you need to decide whether to buy your entire position now or just nibble, with the idea of adding more later if you are right.

Chapter 6 deals with how much money you are going to need. Chapter 12 considers whether to get in all at once or in stages.

There are a few new pieces of information included on Figure 1.4. At the top of the chart is a line labeled Ease of Movement. It is a measurement of just that: how easy or hard is it for a stock to move up or down. Notice that it tends to be above the zero line during advances and below the zero line during declines. At the time of the chart the

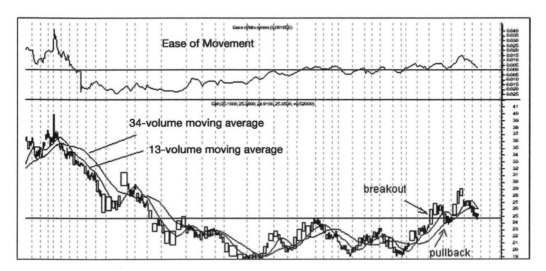

FIGURE 1.4   Other Analytical Tools.

Ease of Movement had crossed into plus territory enough to suggest the stock might be commencing an advance.

Chapter 19 explains the calculation and interpretation of Ease of Movement.

Overlying the prices are a pair of lines that are volume-adjusted moving averages. They are much like traditional moving averages, but they conform to the concepts of Equivolume, which say that heavier volume is more important than lighter volume. The parameters can be changed, but in this case I am using the 13-volume and the 34-volume moving averages. More on that later.

Volume-adjusted moving averages, their construction and interpretation, are explained in Chapter 19.

Notice that the two lines tend to cross one another, with the more volatile line being above the less volatile line during short-term advances, and below it during declines. At the time of this chart they are just going negative; that is, the more volatile line has gone below the less volatile one, after being the other way for the entire advance of about six weeks.

But we were just in the process of buying some of the stock. Let's take a closer look at that buying process. In Figure 1.5, I asked the computer to enlarge the data.

It would have been good to buy the stock earlier, on the first sign of strength, say, right after the first of the three gaps pointed out on the chart. But there were two problems. One was the fact that the stock had not broken out. It was, in fact, approaching

FIGURE 1.5 The Buying Process.

the old resistance level, which had a long history of turning the stock back down. The second was the shape of the box after the gap. It was so square as to suggest sellers were lying in wait just above that level. It made the gap look suspiciously like an exhaustion gap rather than a breakaway gap.

Box sizes and shapes are explained in Chapter 5. Gaps are wonderful indicators (see Chapter 13).

A week later there was another move that might have been tempting. Again there was a gap, and again volume increased. Moreover, the box shape indicated less difficulty in moving the price. However, there was still no powerful move through a resistance level, no breakout. In retrospect it would have gotten us into a winner earlier, but at the time we did not know it was going to break out.

In Chapter 4 we talk about anticipation and its pitfalls.

Two weeks elapse before we are again brought to attention by the action of the stock. Again it leaves a small gap behind, and again volume becomes very heavy. Moreover, it has wide trading range—it is a tall Equivolume box. But the most important feature of the day is that it penetrates the top of the consolidation area, and it does so decisively. It is not a small penetration on light volume, which would be suspect. It shows us power and determination. This looks like a strong indication to buy the stock.

But where do we buy it? If we were watching it very closely during the trading day we might have been aware that it was breaking out, that volume was increasing, and that the range was starting to expand. If so, we might have bought at least a partial position somewhere below the high of the day. It is more likely, though, that we would buy it the next day, after seeing the complete data for the breakout day. As noted earlier, by doing so we would be ignoring the fact that most breakouts are followed by a lighter-volume pullback before continuing higher.

Usually it pays to wait and see if a stock is going to pull back some before buying. I like to see a pullback and then the start of a new strengthening as a signal to buy. It is a more conservative approach that means sometimes missing opportunities, but it also helps to get a better price on many trades. The best approach would have been to follow the stock down as it pulled back, with a stop buy order just above the highs. Then, as soon as it turned up it would be bought. The number of shares is, of course, a function of how much money we are using in the account, and what part of it we are going to put in any single situation

Account size is discussed in Chapter 9. Size of trades and allocations to each issue are also discussed in Chapter 9.

We might even put on a second position on the pullback after the next advance. By stair stepping into a stock, we are changing from just a single position trade to a campaign. We are committing more than the normal amount of money to a single stock and turning a trade into what I like to call a play.

Refer to Chapter 12 ("A Play, Not a Position").

So we contact our broker and place a buy order.

Choosing a broker is covered in Chapter 9. Types of orders are suggested in Chapters 9, 10, and 11. Read about stops to use when entering the market in Chapter 10.

PROTECTING THE POSITION

Using one of the two methods suggested, we now have a full long position in General Motors. But that does not mean we can just sit back and watch. In buying that stock we have assumed a risk. Now we need to limit the dangers imposed by that risk. In other words, we have to protect ourselves from a big loss. That calls for immediately placing another type of stop order, a protective stop. I believe that every position should be guarded by a stop order, or, if the investor has the fortitude and the position is too large for a feasible stop order, at least a mental stop that is obeyed.

Protective stops are discussed in Chapter 11.

In that the $23.50 area was the resistance to upward moves before it was penetrated, it is logical to look for that level as a new support level. Old resistance very often becomes new support. In fact, the pullback after the breakout went to just above that level. I would look at the stock and decide that I would want to continue to hold it as long as it held above that level. But a break very much below that would tell me that I had made a bad investment; I was wrong. So I would place a stop sell order at around the $23 level, giving the stock just a little leeway.

This stop order is to protect us from a loss, but it will later, if possible, be moved up so that it protects our profits in the same way. It is a trailing stop, but it is not placed on a percentage basis; it is placed on a logical basis. There is a point, at all times, at which we would have to admit we were wrong and the market was right. If we have been anticipating a further advance but the technical picture says that a decline is under way that is bigger than we had thought likely, it is at that point that we must get out of the way, take whatever loss or gain there is, and look for some other place to be putting our money.

Our stop-loss order is a one-way street. It can be moved higher, but it can never be moved lower. (See Figure 1.6.)

See closing a position in Chapter 11.

FIGURE 1.6 Progressive Stop Orders.

TAKING A PROFIT

As the stock moves higher, we look at the primary trend, which we are attempting to trade, but we make our stop decisions based on the next smaller wave pattern. This allows us to move the stop order higher as the advance progresses, but keeps us from holding the stock if the secondary wave pattern warns us that the primary move is losing momentum.

See Chapter 20 for a discussion on signals from the next larger cycle.

In this very well-behaving stock we are able to move the stop up five times. Each move protects more profit. As long as the secondary wave pattern is giving us a series of higher lows, the stock is acting well, and we want to stay with it.

There comes a time, though, when the move runs out of energy. We see the change in the characteristics of trading in Figure 1.7.

There are other clues that the move may be due to end. The most important is the cause-and-effect relationship, which allows us to determine approximate targets. The width of the base in this stock, General Motors, suggested the move would probably run out of energy quite soon.

Determining targets is covered in Chapter 18.

FIGURE 1.7 Changing Trading Characteristics.

When the stock drops below the prior low we are stopped out, only a little shy of the top of the move. As the stock price drops, the bottom of the ascending channel is penetrated, suggesting the advance is over. Moreover, the volume increases on the downside for the first time since the advance got under way.

Channels and trend lines are explained in Chapter 17. See direction of volume in Chapter 8.

So, now we are out of the stock. Volume has come in on a decline rather than an advance, and General Motors looks as though it may be headed lower. Shall we go short? No! The advance may be over, but we would need to see more evidence before going to the short side. But the short side should not be ignored. It can often produce bigger and quicker profits than the long side. In the next chapter we will look at an example of a short.

CHAPTER 2

A Pair of Shorts

I n the prior chapter we were looking at a profitable purchase of a stock, but we must not forget that stocks go both ways. To some it seems dangerous, confusing, or disloyal to sell a stock, betting that it is going to decline. However, the fact is that stocks go both up and down, and if we trade only one side of the market we are eliminating half our opportunities to make money.

I well remember the 1972–1974 decline, when the markets retreated for 18 straight months, with hardly any worthwhile rallying. That meant that almost all stocks were under pressure. To buy into that condition was extremely dangerous, because even the best stocks were sliding. The day-after-day erosion tended to hurt everybody. But by recognizing that it was a protracted bear market, and attempting to capitalize on it, one could make money even under those conditions.

In later chapters we will be looking at market measurements and market direction. There are times when the market direction is definitely down, and those are the times when being a buyer can be a mistake. Yes, a few stocks may be going up, but the odds are certainly stacked against finding them among the preponderance of losers.

Chapters 20 to 23 deal with market direction forecasting.

THE ARGUMENT FOR GOING SHORT

An argument used for not going short is that with a long position your potential gain is unlimited and your potential loss is only as much as the price of the stock. The reverse is the case when one is short; then the potential gain is limited to the price of the stock, but the potential loss is infinite. Theoretically this is true. But we, as traders, are not going into any stock with the idea of holding it until it goes to zero or infinity. Moreover, we must always use stop orders to protect against excessive losses. So, on that basis, the preceding argument against using the short side of the market is absurd.

I have often been told, "I won't ever go short, because that calls for a margin account with my broker. My grandfather lost his shirt in 1929 because he had a margin account. I do not want to take that kind of risk." Yes, if you want to go short you have to have a margin account. But that does not mean that you are borrowing money. The margin account allows your broker to borrow the stock in order to meet the requirements of delivering stock to the person who bought it from you. But you have not increased your risk by the action. Unless you purposely decide to, you will not be borrowing money to complete the transaction. If you did not have the aforementioned stops, if you did not have extra money in the account, and if the stock went a long distance against you, you could be called for more margin. But the way we are looking at trading in this book, it should never happen. Moreover, the grandfather who lost his shirt was operating on very low initial margin requirements that are not allowed in today's more regulated markets.

In a way, going short could be considered safer than going long. The reason is that stock prices tend to move faster when they are going down than when they are going up. It is just about two to one. In other words, a stock typically drops twice as quickly as it rises. That means that buyers, long a stock, have the potential for the stock to go in their direction slowly or against them rapidly. They have little time to correct their mistakes. In contrast, traders who are short a stock are likely to see the stock go with them rapidly or against them slowly. They have more time to recognize and correct their errors.

As for the thought that selling a stock short is somehow disloyal to the economy, the country, or the corporation, we are not trading stocks to influence their longer-term direction. We are buying stocks or shorting stocks to take advantage of their short-term swings, regardless of their longer-term direction. We should, as traders, have little or no interest in the long-term prospects of a company. A stock is a vehicle for making money.

For all these reasons it is important that the trader be as willing to go short as to go long. He or she must have a margin account, but does not have to become overly aggressive by using borrowed money. To ignore the short side of the market is to eliminate half the opportunities, and to be tempted to buy into markets that are in a decline. It is always better to match your trading to the market's direction. Short selling is sometimes the only way to do so.

EXAMPLE OF A SHORT TRADE

Let's look at an example of a short trade. As shown in Figure 2.1, IBM's stock had been in an uptrend toward the end of 2005. Then, one day in December, it suddenly traded

FIGURE 2.1 Example of a Short Trade.

on much heavier volume and it moved sharply lower. It was moving so fast it even left a gap behind. That is the first indicated gap, on the left side of the chart. That produced a power box to the downside. What qualified that price bar as a power box was that it was the first such jump in volume and trading range in the direction opposite to the direction the stock had been moving. It was an Equivolume entry that stood out as being very unusual, with its wide trading range and its heavy volume.

See Chapter 8 for more on power boxes.

The gap it left behind was another alert that the stock was suddenly turning weak. Moreover, it moved down through the ascending trend line. The stock appeared to be offering us an opportunity to make some money on the short side.

Trend lines are discussed in Chapter 17.

Prior to the power box, we had been seeing volume come in each time the stock moved up, and then less volume each time the stock moved lower. So, until that time the volume was indicating continued strength. That made the down day on heavy volume look particularly significant. The gap down would be classified as a breakaway gap because the box after the gap was much wider than the box before the gap.

See gaps in Chapter 13.

Is there reason enough here to put on a short position? There are pluses and minuses certainly. On the negative side is the fact that the top is quite narrow in terms of volume. We know that a wide top is more likely to generate a big decline than is a narrow top. Second, by the time the big box to the downside is made there has already been quite a large decline. It makes one wonder if the move has already gone too far too fast. At the least it would look as though some rallying would be likely before going lower. If that occurred, it would somewhat broaden the volume width of the top, thereby justifying more downside.

Chapter 18 discusses volume cycles.

But the positives are also apparent, and compelling. The biggest factor is, of course, the big downward box that we have classified as a power box. Second, we have the down day, which suggests weakness. Because the power box has broken the ascending trend line, the implication is that we are going to see a down move. It may be overdone on a short-term basis, but it looks as though it is going to move lower, even if it has a rally first. So our intention should be to go short at an advantageous price, after the stock has had a chance to rally a little and broaden the top. It would be tempting to just jump in, but patience usually is more rewarding. There is absolutely no reason we must go short this stock. There will certainly be other opportunities coming along. On any day there are dozens of stocks producing big boxes, many of which could be called power boxes. But we do not want to pass up a good opportunity. So, let us call this a potential short sale at this time.

Over the next three weeks the stock drifted somewhat lower before a rally. This is longer than we often see for the secondary test to develop. But it helped us in this case, because it broadened the consolidation. Ideally we would wait until the completion of the countertrend rally before going short. If we had gone into the short on that first light-volume up move instead, we would have been stopped out within a week, which would have led to a very small loss. That hypothetical loser is enclosed in an ellipse on the next chart (Figure 2.2), and the trades are distinguished by question marks. But that should not have deterred us from reestablishing the short position when the conditions looked right a few days later.

The new sign of weakness is evident further to the right, as volume and price range have increased, and the decline has appeared to resume. It looks a like a good time to put on the short position. By this time the danger level is also quite evident—the highs of the rally were approached three times; just above that point looks like a good place to put in a stop-loss order. If IBM rose above that level, it would be showing a renewal of strength, suggesting we were wrong in going short. That stop is going to have to stay there or be moved lower as the future unfolds, but we must never move it up. (See Figure 2.3.)

Protective stops are discussed in Chapter 11.

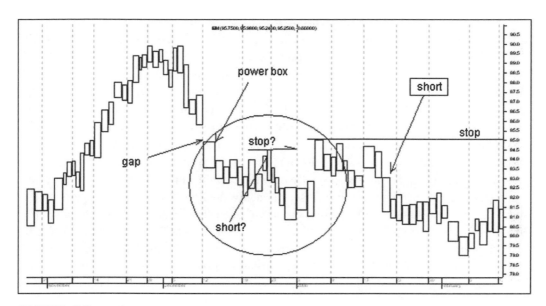

FIGURE 2.2   A Closer View.

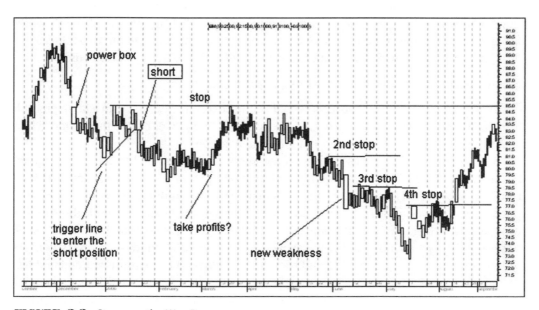

FIGURE 2.3   Stops on the Way Down.

After we established a short position, the stock did move lower. Then it built a small base and moved up with better volume. That might have been enough to cause us to take the profits on the position, depending on how aggressively we had followed the decline with our stop. There is really nothing wrong with that, except that our intention was to be using the large wave pattern, and this may be just a smaller wave within that pattern. But there is enough evidence to suggest a rally could carry quite a distance and jeopardize the existing profits. If we did take the profit at that time, we would not have been willing to go back in at the next big down, which I have marked as "new weakness." To do so would have meant going into a position late in a move, rather than at its inception.

Assuming, though, that we stayed with the position, the stop level would not have been penetrated, but it was very close. Then the decline resumed, and again volume came in on the downside. From then on down, each time it dropped though a support level we were alerted we were entering a new trading zone. We then watched for the countertrend rally that would define the top of the new zone, and moved our stop down to just above the top of that rally. Now, instead of protecting against a loss, we were guarding a profit. As the decline progressed we felt that the decline was becoming a little aged, and were therefore willing to move the stops closer and closer.

The rally with the big gap just before the fourth stop level was particularly disconcerting. Volume increased to the upside, and a big gap was left behind. It had the earmarks of an important reversal from the downtrend, and prompted an even more cautious stance in which the stop was moved in so close that any undue strength would bring about a closing of the short position. The next rally might be enough to take us out, depending on just how close we put the stop. If not, the next rally certainly did.

Profit-taking stops are illustrated in Chapter 11.

As we see in Figure 2.4, the stop served its purpose, and kept us from a large possible loss. As it was, the next up move in IBM was a convincing power box to the upside, which was the precursor of a large and profitable long position.

Remember, all the signals we are accustomed to using on the buy side work equally well on the sell side. We will be looking for breakouts, power boxes, gaps, consolidations, trend lines, and reversals in just the same manner as we look for those characteristics on stocks we want to buy. That is not to say, though, that bottoms look the same as tops. As we will see later, particularly in market averages rather than individual issues, bottoms and tops are not exactly the same. Lows on a market, and often on a stock, are more likely to be sharp, exciting, and traumatic. Tops tend to be more gradual and less emotional. As we go along, we will recognize, at times, that there is a difference and that we need to look for that difference. In the later chapters we will, when it is appropriate, note those differences and therefore the types of signals we will want to see on both the buy side and the sell side.

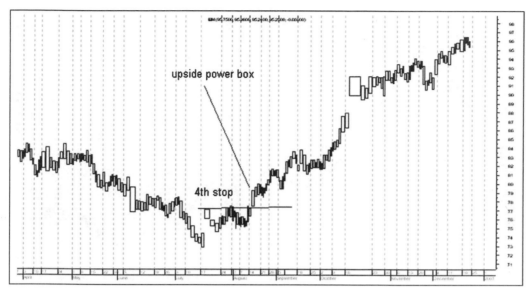

FIGURE 2.4 The End of the Decline.

ANOTHER SUCCESSFUL SHORT

Figure 2.5 shows the decline in Toll Brothers' stock in 2005 and 2006. In this example the position lasted for a long time. It could, in fact, have been used as a longer-term play rather than just a single position.

Chapter 12 discusses multiple positions.

Throughout the decline, it never made a significant higher high; they were all progressively lower. That meant the stop price could be successfully lowered time after time, protecting more and more profits. When it did finally turn up, almost a year later, very little of the profit was left on the table. Rarely will a position last so long, but in this case it was very worthwhile. In that time the stock lost half its value.

It should be understood that these examples have been chosen because they worked very well. Moreover, the placing of orders is somewhat arbitrary. As you do more trading you will develop a feel for placing and moving stops, which is the key to maximizing your profits while limiting your risks. We can capitalize upon the fact that stocks tend to act in certain ways, but we cannot ever know for sure that they will do what we expect. That is the biggest reason for using stop orders, not only to get us out, but also to get us in. Moreover, we need to use any other useful tools that will swing the odds in our favor.

FIGURE 2.5 The Big Decline in Toll Brothers' Stock.

All the tools we will be using are technical. You will not read about earnings or dividends. There will be no sections on government reports or corporate news. Management or products will be of no interest to us. So maybe the first thing we should do is look at technical analysis, and see why it should be our method of approaching a trading program. That is the subject of the next chapter.

CHAPTER 3

Why Technical Analysis?

Buying a stock because it has a good story is easy. It is a warm and comfortable feeling to own a stock because you have learned, perhaps through a great deal of hard digging, or perhaps as a casual suggestion from someone else, that the company is bound to do well. Perhaps it has a hot new product, or perhaps it has dynamic new management. Maybe the talk is that it is just about to be acquired, or it is going to show great earnings. The especially comfortable feeling comes when it is a company you know and patronize, such as a retail store or a fast food outlet. Buying stocks, especially for a novice, is an experience that is filled with apprehension, so anything that can be done to reduce that apprehension seems like a good idea. Knowing a happy story about a stock helps to bring on that comfort we crave.

Buying a stock because it has a great-looking chart is far more difficult. That is even truer if the story you hear about it is dismal. If nobody likes the stock, if the news is terrible, if the earnings have been poor, if the management is suspect, if your broker is not recommending it, if the overall market has been plunging, it becomes a nearly insurmountable deluge to move against. Yet, it is often under just such circumstances that the best opportunities first emerge. Therefore, it is necessary to develop a comfort level, based on a thorough knowledge of the technical methods being used.

The reason that stocks so often are the best buys when they are the most dismal stories is that the market does not trade based on the present; it trades based on the future. It is a game in which we are always trying to be ahead of the other guy. For the earnings to be going to go higher, they first have to be low. Knowing when they are as low as they are going to go is not knowledge we are likely to be able to acquire. But there are people out there who know better than we do when that turn in earnings may be barely visible on the misty horizon. We do not have to know when the turn occurs; we just have to know when someone else thinks the turn is starting to occur. That person, or actually that big group of people, will start to acquire the stock, knowing things are going to be better. And when they do that, they tip their hand. They create price movement and they generate volume. If we are astute and observant, we can often see that action. It emerges as a typical action. The observation of the things others are doing in the marketplace is the basis of technical analysis.

DISCOUNTING

Technicians are aware that there is a huge difference between supply and demand for a company's products or services and supply and demand for a company's stock. Often the two types of demand seem to be unrelated, or at best related vaguely. If we really want to find a relationship between stock action and company action, we need to look for a time offset. Since a stock is a reflection of a discounting of the likely future events, it is often observed that all the best news comes out at the top and all the worst news comes out at the bottom. When I see a piece of news that has the traders excited, I like to look at what the stock has been doing. That tells me whether the street has already been in the process of discounting that news (i.e., factoring the news into the stock price). The old Wall Street advice to buy on the rumor and sell on the news has validity. Those who are close to the company have known for a long time when things have been going badly or going well. That knowledge is reflected in the price action and the volume of trading. So, as a technician, one needs to try to recognize and identify that action, and capitalize upon it.

Technical analysis is not rocket science, nor is buying and selling stocks. That is really the problem. The stock market is far more complex. The nice thing about a scientific pursuit, however complex, is that rigid rules can be established. The force of gravity is measurable and predictable, and exact and unchangeable values can be assigned, depending on the circumstances. Acceleration can be forecast, orbits can be calculated, and velocities are predetermined. Barring the uncertainty of Dr. Heisenberg, for most practical purposes it becomes a clockwork universe.

By contrast, the prediction of stock market action and the art of investing are far more complex because they deal with human emotions rather than with scientific laws. A falling object, physicists tell us, accelerates at 32 feet per second. A falling stock drops at a terrifying and dizzying, but unpredictable rate. It is as though we see the results of a scientific experiment, but do not know what the experiment itself has been. However, by observing the results of the experiment we can make some deductions about the procedure that produced those results. When we see the action of a stock or a group of stocks, we can gather an understanding of what probably has caused that action.

However, the really important information is not the cause of the activity, but the activity itself. The one thing that the technician has working for him or her is the fact that under similar circumstances people tend to react in similar ways. In other words, human responses are predictable. Readers may be familiar with the "Foundation" series of science fiction books written by Isaac Asimov. His protagonist, Hari Seldon, was a psychohistorian. Asimov introduced here a wonderful concept, which he called psychohistory. He said that the actions of a single individual could not be accurately predicted, but the actions of a very large group of people could be predicted, because, as a group, they would in general react to the same situation in the same way. Market technicians are psychohistorians. They realize that all market movement is a result of human psychology, and that large groups of people are predictable. So, the next time you are on an airline trip and the person sitting next to you asks, "What do you do?" instead of saying, "I look at charts and try to predict what stock prices will do," you can answer, "I am a psychohistorian." As a result of the blank stare that follows, you should be able to get some sleep on the flight.

THE TECHNICIAN'S ADVANTAGE

The great advantage of technical analysis is that it simplifies information and removes extraneous information. If a stock is not going to be moving because of news items or is unpredictable in response to news items, then there is no need to pay attention to the news items. It reduces the workload and eliminates unimportant and useless factors. Actually, of course, all the news items are included in the technical data, so they are not really being ignored; they are being assimilated. But the market, rather than the analyst, is doing the assimilation. You may not know if a piece of news is good or bad for the supply and demand balance for the company's stock, but the market does know. It is immediately reflected in the price and the volume. I try to shield myself from the news. I feel that the market has already looked at the news, evaluated it, reacted emotionally to it, and included it in the price of the stock. If I listen to a single bit of information, and take it into consideration in making a buy or sell decision, I am giving that bit of information double weight, because it is already reflected in the price and volume data. I believe in the efficient market hypothesis, but my own modified version. The market is extremely efficient in reflecting everything that is known about a stock, but only after that information has been processed by the millions of human brains that consider it. The price of a stock is not a reflection of the raw facts, but a reflection of the facts as interpreted by the investing public. Therefore, psychohistory.

THE EFFECT OF FUNDAMENTALS

Does all of this mean that there is no relationship between stock price and company value? Of course not. In the long run, companies that have good business plans, good management, good earnings, and needed products or services tend to move higher. Businesses that are failing, that have poor management, and that have obsolete products tend to go down. But the catch in that statement is the phrase "in the long run." In the long run, we will be in and out of the stock a dozen times. In between, the up and down waves may be caused by the fundamentals, but those moves are very difficult to predict from a fundamental standpoint. So, the shorter the time frame of trading, the more difficult it becomes to base decisions on fundamentals. That brings us to the technical picture. It reflects the supply and demand for a company's stock rather that the supply and demand for the goods or services produced by that company. And that is what we want to trade: the stock, not the company.

Technical analysis is not a matter of recognizing interesting patterns to which names have been attached, such as head and shoulders or saucer bottoms. That is certainly a manifestation of the discipline—it allows one to quickly describe a type of activity. However, underlying the formations are the dynamics. A stock tends to make a triple top because the sellers reemerge at the same approximate level. Volume tends to decrease across the top as the sellers and buyers become exhausted. Power boxes come in because something has radically changed in a stock. Levels are penetrated because the buyers or sellers have gained control. There is a reason for the action, and we need to understand that reason. It helps us to make better decisions.

ELIMINATING EMOTIONS

Another reason for relying on technical analysis is that it allows one to be more realistic and more detached. That leads to less emotional decisions, and less emotional decisions tend to be better decisions. Yes, the price of a stock is a delicate balance between fear and greed, but we as technicians should stand aside and observe that balancing act rather than contribute to it. We should recognize the fear, and when it is unreasoning fear it is usually a time to go in the other direction. Similarly, when everyone appears to be fearlessly buying it is probably a time to be selling. Technical analysis allows us to be contrarians.

Being a contrarian does not mean always going against the crowd, however. It means recognizing extremes and becoming a contrarian at that time. There are a number of indicators explained in other chapters that allow us to recognize those emotional extremes. Being a contrarian at all times would be disastrous. Most of the time the adage that "the trend is your friend" holds true. It is at the end of a trend that one needs to recognize that it has been carried too far.

The reasons for using technical analysis, then, are efficiency and relevancy. We are only looking at what is important, yet we are, indirectly, looking at far more information than could ever be studied with a fundamental approach. The fundamentalist could look at all the public data, but would be unable to factor in the millions of decisions based on extraneous factors. Moreover, even if all of those factors could be known, there would be no way of knowing whether each was a positive or a negative, or how much weight each should be given. But the market is a mechanism that does all that for us, finally delivering just two pertinent pieces of information: price and volume.

CHAPTER 4

The Market Is Always Right

Some years back a long-time friend accompanied me to my office, where we were talking about my work and at the same time observing what was happening in the marketplace. As I watched the prices change I said, "Oh, damn that market!"—whereupon my friend mumbled something I didn't hear. I asked him to repeat it and he said, "Anthropomorphism—the attributing of human characteristics to inanimate objects. That's what you were just doing. You were damning the market."

He was right, of course; that is what we often do. We think of the stock market as a benevolent or a vindictive entity, depending on whether it is going with us or against us. In our minds the market becomes a humanlike force. And that may be a part of the problem. In saying the market is always right we are insinuating it has an ability to be right or wrong. But if the market is a nonhuman thing like a rock or a tree, or perhaps more aptly like a gigantic machine, it cannot be right or wrong. It just is.

Yet the anthropomorphic approach has validity in a way. The market is not an individual, but is a consensus of millions of individuals. Fundamental analysts try to eliminate the human element from the marketplace, saying that price movements are the result of earnings, dividends, management, products, competition, and hundreds of other measurable factors. The technician concedes that the fundamental factors that underlie the market are the driving force in determining price, but only after they are processed by human minds. And it is those human minds that make the market seem like a gigantic person. So, for our use, we will continue to think of the market as a person, but an omnipotent person, who cannot, by definition, be wrong.

BECOMING OBSERVERS

If, then, we are dealing with a force that is almost godlike in that it cannot be wrong, then we must put ourselves in the role of observers rather than determinants. We cannot dictate the direction or extent of price movements; we can only observe them and try to go with them. Obviously, this is done for convenience and effectiveness. The markets are not actually godlike. They are accurately reflecting every human input. There are millions of people, worldwide, who are all buying and selling stocks based on their individual reasons. A seller may have heard a rumor, true or false, about the stock, or he may just need to get some money to pay his taxes. He may have bought the stock a lot cheaper, and fears giving the profit back, or he may have bought the stock a week ago at a higher price and is suddenly overcome by fear it will go lower. Each of these reasons, and hundreds more, go into the mix, and add to the selling pressure on the stock. But there is also the other side of the market. There are buyers who might have heard the same rumor and did not believe it, or who just got a tax refund and needed to put some money to work, or thought the pullback of the past week was a buying opportunity. These and a myriad of other decisions are distilled by the market to just two simple pieces of information: the price of the stock and the volume of trading in the stock. It is a constantly changing and very delicate equilibrium, balancing all the accumulated greed against all the accumulated fear and arriving at a consensus, which is called a trade.

The fundamentalist tries to look at all of the information that is being fed into that equation and decide what the effect will be. There are two big problems with this. The first is that there can be no way the analyst can ever see all of the necessary information. Even if one could, it would be so overwhelming as to be insurmountable. The second problem is that even if one knows the pertinent information, there is no way to know how it will be assessed by the minds of investors. We have all seen the effect of earnings reports on a stock. It can be a great report and be considered bullish, but often the street thinks it is not good enough and drops the price of the stock. Also, it has been anticipated, discussed, forecast, disputed, and discounted for days or weeks before the report is released. All those actions have altered the psychological response to the reality. Therefore, the response becomes virtually unpredictable.

Figure 4.1 shows a late 2006 chart of Microsoft. Note the big rise and the subsequent drop. Right at the top of that move, Microsoft announced a large release of new and exciting products. That sounds bullish, but it proved to be the end of the advance. The stock dropped sharply, rallied once more, and then went substantially lower.

Does this lead us to the attitude that the market is a random and unpredictable mechanism? No, because even if we cannot possibly predict the human response to a deluge of fundamental data, we can observe the synthesis of all the reactions to those data. By looking at the output of the computation rather than the input, we have greatly simplified the problem. Instead of thousands of fundamental factors, we have reduced them to

FIGURE 4.1 Microsoft Chart.

just two technical pieces of information: price and volume. It is the interpretation of that information that is the subject of this book and that is the basis of technical analysis.

We personalize the market, though we often do as I did; we blame it. The blame must fall on ourselves, however, if we make decisions that do not pay off. The market truly is always right. If we fail, it is because we have failed to correctly interpret the market and its swings. I have a client and friend who is also a bellwether for me. After the markets have been in a move that seems to have gone on far too long without a correction, and I am frustrated by the fact that my work suggests a turn but it has not occurred, I often receive a phone call from him, in which he tells me that "they" are acting insanely and prices are being driven to ridiculous levels by "them." When that happens, I know we are just about at the turning point. He is a professional, and he is a very successful investor, but he becomes incensed with "them." He is just venting his frustration, because actually he is well aware that he cannot fight "them." He has to go with the market, even if he feels it is beating him up. His complaint about "them" is another form of humanizing the market. It gives him someone to blame.

Which takes us back to the title of this chapter; if the market is always right, then there is really no one to blame but ourselves. The market is telling us a story. We need to listen to that story and try to interpret its implications. As it unfolds, we can often see where the story is going and take advantage of that knowledge. But if we try to second-guess the plot too far in advance, we are likely to be wrong. The most important thing we know about the story is its general direction. The short-term twists and turns are all leading in one direction, and that direction is likely to continue. If we can correctly interpret the direction the story is taking us, we can be successful in forecasting the outcome.

ANTICIPATION

Let me tell you about a poodle named Blue Chip. He is 85 pounds of canine intelligence. In fact, he is one of the smartest dogs I have ever encountered, and he allows us to live with him. When Chip was a youngster, it was decided that he should attend obedience school. As is usual, the instructor would stand in the center of the training arena, and the owners and their dogs would form a circle around her. Then she would train the owners on how to train their dogs. She would say, "Sit your dogs," "Stand your dogs," or "Tell your dogs to heel," and the owners would issue the instructions and the dogs were supposed to follow the commands. Chip was terrible! This genius dog, who had been house-trained in one day, was flunking obedience school! When he was supposed to be sitting he would stand, and when he was supposed to be standing he would heel. It took his less astute owners a while to realize that he was not dumb; he was too smart. Instead of listening to his owners, he had eliminated the middleman and was listening to the instructor. That put him out of phase with the group. He was anticipating too far into the future, and it was getting him into trouble.

Once the problem was identified, it was easy to convince Chip he should be paying attention to his owner, or at least he should humor his owner and not try to second-guess the instructions. Often I think we are like Chip, but we correct our problems less easily. We try to be smarter than the market, and we therefore second-guess market moves too far in advance. It can, as with Chip, put us out of phase.

The classic type of second-guessing is the belief that a change of direction is imminent and acting on that belief before it actually is signaled. Most often we do that when a stock has been in a decline, and it seems as though it could not possibly go any lower. But the stock has not yet told us it is going up, even if it is acting as though it is through going down. Remember, there are three possible directions: up, down, and sideways. We often forget the sideways move as a possibility. Look at Figure 4.2, of Blockbuster in 2005 and early 2006.

The stock made a heavy-volume low, which had the look of an important support emerging. Two months later it went back near to that level and tested it on light volume. Then it started to strengthen. At that point one would have been tempted to second-guess the move, and buy. But in reality all we knew was that the decline seemed to be ending. The stock had not yet given a sign of strength at the swing level we were anticipating trading. We were looking for the bigger move, like the mirror of the prior decline.

FIGURE 4.2 Blockbuster Chart.

In this case, we would have eventually been proven right, but only after an extension of the consolidation. That would have meant our money was idle for another two months. Moreover, we had taken the risk that the consolidation would lead to a further decline, which would actually be about twice as likely. It might have acted like Geron Corporation, shown in Figure 4.3.

The real buy signal in both examples was not seen until the stock moved above resistance, saying that it was no longer in a sideways consolidation; it had entered an advancing phase. In later chapters we look at better ways of interpreting tops and bottoms, using a more effective charting method than the bar chart shown in Figures 4.1, 4.2, and 4.3.

Yes, the market is always right, so we should not argue with it. In future chapters we will see how to use stop orders to make sure we acknowledge the times when we are wrong and the market is right. We will see how volume can tell us price direction. We will learn about consolidations, and support and resistance levels. We will see how, by understanding the larger picture—the overall market—we can be more successful.

CHOOSING YOUR TOOLS

An immense number of technical tools and methods are available. In fact, there are so many that it becomes confusing, and confusion leads to poor decisions or, often,

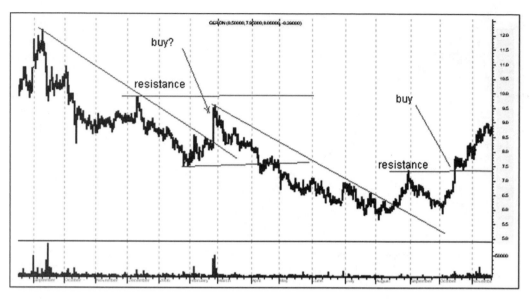

FIGURE 4.3 Geron Chart.

inaction. For that reason it is necessary to limit your tools and rely on them. We will be looking at a number of techniques that have been standbys for many years. For example, one could use bar charts, point-and-figure charts, candlestick charts, Equivolume charts, or line charts. We will be using Equivolume charts. In explaining the methods I have invented and developed over the years, I often tell audiences: "If I give you a watch, you are going to know what time it is; but if I give you three watches, you are just going to be confused." These methods are cohesive and interrelated, and should not require the use of any tools other than those contained in this book.

In the chapters that follow, we look at the methods I have developed and used for a number of decades. They range from volume-adjusted moving averages and Ease of Movement studies to volume cycles. Later we will look at the Arms Index, also known as the Trading Index (TRIN), and other ways of ascertaining the direction of the market itself. I use, almost exclusively, methods that I personally invented and explored. I do not claim they are the best or the only useful methods, but they work for me, and they should work for you.

The cornerstone of my methodology is the study of volume, and the basis of the trading methods we are using is Equivolume. In the next chapter we take a look at this powerful charting method.

CHAPTER 5

Equivolume Charts

I f you were playing golf with Tiger Woods, would you give him a three-stroke advantage? Of course not. If you were crossing the Atlantic in a sailboat, would you leave your compass behind? Never. Would you start on a cross-country car trip without seeing how much gas is in the tank? Certainly not. Would you try to interpret the action of the stock market without knowing the volume? I hope not. When the stock market closes for the day, two pieces of information are all that remains: price and volume. Every decision, every whim, every rumor, every announcement, and every merger has been evaluated and distilled to just those two basic data. Why would anyone choose to ignore half the available information?

When you compete in the stock market you are up against the best in the business. It is like playing golf against Tiger Woods. You are going to need every advantage available to you. When you navigate your way through the ripples, waves, and tides of price swings, you will need a good compass to reach your objective. When you drive along that road, which you hope will lead to wealth, you need to know how much energy is available to you. In the stock market, the amount of gas in the tank is evidenced by the volume of trading. Yet volume is often ignored or forgotten.

THE IMPORTANCE OF VOLUME

But is volume really that important? I believe it is. Price tells us what is happening, but volume tells us *how* it is happening. It gives us an insight into the emotions that are underlying price movement. A price rise on heavy volume is far more meaningful than a similar advance on light trading. It tells us that there are many willing buyers pushing the price. Obviously, with every buyer there is a seller, so there are also many sellers in the marketplace, but they are selling at progressively higher levels as the advance progresses. The heavy volume is reflecting an increased demand for the stock. Without the volume information, we would not be aware of that important detail. Yet many traders use charts that do not contain volume in any form. We see that primarily with people who use candlestick charts, line charts, or point-and-figure charts, but some bar charts also do not have the volume histogram across the bottom margin.

BAR CHARTS

Figure 5.1 shows a typical bar chart. It represents a three-month period in the history of Goodyear Tire's stock. Each small vertical bar depicts one day of trading, and there are two little horizontal ticks attached to each bar. The one to the left is the level at which the stock opened trading for the day; the one to the right is the level where it closed for the day.

Across the bottom of the chart are a series of vertical lines, each representing the trading volume for the day above it. On this type of chart the horizontal dimension is time, while the vertical dimension is price. So, time is a constant. By putting a ruler across the chart, horizontally, a person could measure equal amounts of time.

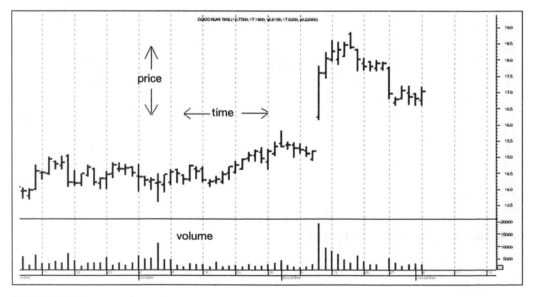

FIGURE 5.1 Typical Bar Chart.

It is possible, but sometimes a little difficult, to recognize which volume posting relates to which price posting. We can see on this example that there are a few days where volume is very low, and others where volume is very high. The one day with the highest volume obviously goes with the huge up price move. So, volume is telling us something useful on this chart. But there is a lot more to the interpretation of volume than just that. To interpret volume properly, though, we need a better way of seeing what is happening. That better way is called Equivolume charting.

ADVANTAGE OF EQUIVOLUME CHARTS

As we noted earlier, the price is one part of the chart, and the volume is carried, almost as an afterthought, as a separate piece of information, a histogram across the bottom of the page. Many years ago, while driving home one afternoon and thinking about a recent trade, I conceived the idea of moving the volume up off the lower margin and including it in the price, as a single posting. To do so, I would have to abandon time as a constant along the lower margin, and make each posting a rectangle, with the volume the width of each posting and the high and low remaining as they were on the bar chart. The idea led to many months of experimentation and the production of many charts in order to try to understand whether the method would be helpful. The result led to my first book, *Profits in Volume*, which explained the new methodology that I called Equivolume.

Figure 5.2 repeats the same three-month period for the same stock, Goodyear Tire, but changed to an Equivolume chart.

Suddenly we have a very different picture. But remember, we are not looking at any new information. It is just the same information depicted in a different manner. There is never any additional information available to us, just different ways of looking at it. But what a difference! I have indicated three boxes, one very small, one very large, and one fairly normal in size. They are each just one day of trading, yet they look very dissimilar. That is because they are showing us, graphically, the great variety in both price range and volume that are seen on just this short history of a single stock. Moreover, as we look at any box on the chart, we are seeing a true picture of supply and demand for the stock on that trading day. The size of each box indicates how much trading interest, in general, there was on that day. The height of the box shows the distance between the highest and lowest price levels touched that day, and the width is telling us how many shares traded. The overall shape combines those two factors to tell us how easy or hard it was for price to move. I like to picture it as two battling armies. There are times when they are far apart and sniping at each other in a desultory manner. There are other times when the trenches are close together and there is hand-to-hand combat. There are times when one army is charging and the other is falling back in disarray. The box sizes and

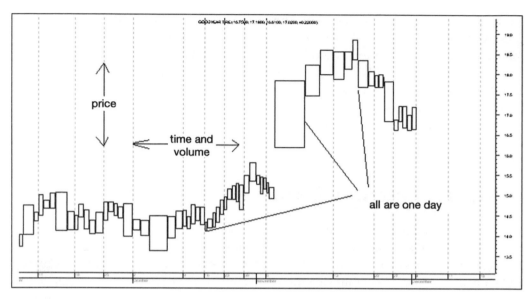

FIGURE 5.2 Typical Equivolume Chart.

shapes and the direction and extent of movement are imparting all that information, and much more.

As we go along, you will learn that there is a great deal of information conveyed by these charts. Some are the same methods as those used on bar charts, but adapted to the Equivolume technique. Others are interpretations based entirely on the Equivolume technique.

ALL DAYS ARE NOT THE SAME

I mentioned that we had abandoned time as a constant along the horizontal axis. At first that may seem like a problem, but it is actually an advantage, and it has a basis in reason. Because each day is represented by a single box, it is simple to know the time frame, and also the dates are shown across the bottom of the chart. But it becomes immediately apparent in looking at any chart that a month, for example, can be quite narrow or quite wide, depending on how heavy the volume is during that month. So, when we have very little trading we have narrower (less dramatic) postings, and when things are really happening the postings are wider. That is as it should be.

I often make the statement that the market does not know what time it is. That is because time is a human measurement, not a stock market measurement. For example, if the market is closed for the weekend, no stock changes hands; therefore, nothing has happened, even though time has passed. We have always subconsciously acknowledged that fact by not leaving spaces on our bar charts for Saturday and Sunday. We put the Monday posting right up against the prior Friday's posting, since the weekend is meaningless. The Equivolume chart is an extension of that concept. If time is not a stock market measurement, what is? Obviously, volume. The heavier the volume, the more that is happening. Looking at the Equivolume chart and the three different boxes I have indicated as all being individual days, indubitably the wider boxes are more important than the narrower boxes. Equivolume capitalizes on that difference.

The volume-based x-axis has other advantages. If we can measure, directly on the chart, the amount of volume in a base or a move, we can observe that there is a cause-and-effect relationship that is volume based rather than time based. That leads to being able to establish price targets and also to recognize volume-based cycles.

The Equivolume method not only allows one to abandon the bar chart, replacing it with a more informative display, but it also allows the establishment of likely price targets without having to use point-and-figure charts.

Does this mean, then, that analysts will have to spend their time drawing these unique charts? Not necessarily. When I first developed this method, I had no choice but to draw my own charts. In my first book, *Profits in Volume*, I went into great detail as to how to calculate the proper volume parameter for each stock, since different stocks had different volume characteristics. It is still a worthwhile learning experience to draw a few of your own charts. It provides a feel for how price and volume interact, and a deeper understanding of the interplay of these two forces. Anyone wishing to know how to do so may want to go back to the aforementioned book for the details. But today's technology has removed all the drudgery.

One of the big problems that cropped up when drawing Equivolume charts by hand was that, over time, some stocks changed their volume characteristics so much that I had to throw out the old charts and start again with a different volume scale. Similarly, as prices changed they would sometimes run off the top or the bottom of the page, and the chart would have to be discarded and redrawn. It became a huge job just to keep up with a few stocks.

COMPUTER-DRAWN CHARTS

With the computer programs now available it has become extremely easy to look at virtually any number of issues in a short time. Since the charts are recalculated each time they are selected, there is never any trouble with changes in normal volume or changing price ranges. The computer program makes the proper adjustments. What used to be a job taking many hours is now done instantly.

Moreover, all of the other indicators that we will be looking at can be immediately accessed. Moving averages, even volume-adjusted moving averages, are instantly added to the display. Ease of Movement is added to the chart with the click of a mouse.

The example in Figure 5.2 looked at a very small time frame for a stock. In reality, we will usually be looking at longer time spans in doing our interpretation. Figure 5.3 shows a typical daily-based Equivolume chart. That is, each rectangle represents one day of trading, and we have asked the computer to compress the display so that we are looking at the past six months of activity. This happens to be Boeing in late 2006.

Boeing is a heavy trader every day, and has immense institutional participation. Therefore, there tends to be more of a uniformity of box sizes than might be seen in a thinly traded issue. Nevertheless, notice the variety of Equivolume boxes we see here. It is apparent there are times when the trading becomes much more intense, and other times when things quiet down. Also, notice that there is a correlation between heavier volume and more price movement. It is possible to better see the areas of strength and weakness with this type of chart. It also is seen that the volume tends to be heavier in the direction of the trend and dries up on countertrend moves. One can also start to get the feel for the cycles, which, as we will see in Chapter 18, are volume dependent rather than time dependent. See, you are already reading and interpreting a chart based on the Equivolume methodology!

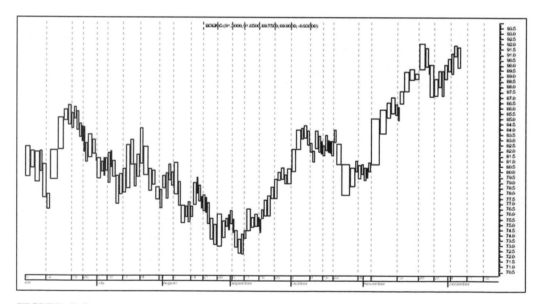

FIGURE 5.3 A Longer-Term Equivolume Chart.

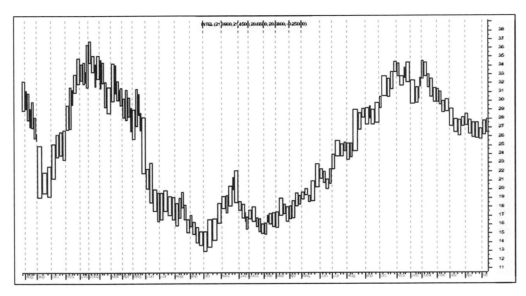

FIGURE 5.4 Weekly Chart of Intel.

OTHER TIME FRAMES

So far we have looked at daily-based charts, but neither the method nor the technology precludes using other parameters. A day trader may want to subscribe to a real-time data feed and look at 10-minute charts. A longer-term investor may want to look at weekly charts in order to gain a better perspective. In both cases the methods put forth in these pages are still valid. The day trader will find bigger shifts in box size, while the investor looking at a weekly chart will be seeing less variety in entry size. Figure 5.4, for example, is a weekly-based chart, covering about three years of trading in Intel from late 2001 to early 2004. Notice that the boxes are quite similar to one another because of the smoothing effect of bunching the data. Nevertheless, although less dramatic, the variety of box shapes and sizes is informative. Particularly note the fact that the heavier-volume weeks tend to be on the downside during the declines and tend to be on the upside during the advances. The change of direction, just to the left of the center of the chart, shows an obvious shift in volume emphasis and alerts us the stock may be starting to turn to an advancing phase.

It is the change in volume and trading range characteristics that leads us to the most important tool we have for initiating a trade, the power box. While not the only tool that can tell us when to go long or short a stock, it is extremely important and reliable. So, let's gather together the tools we are going to need in order to start trading, and after that we can go looking for power boxes.

CHAPTER 6

Getting Ready to Trade

If you are going to be a market trader, and if you are going to follow the technical ideas in this book, there are a number of things you are going to need, and some you are going to have to pay for. But there are also a number of things you not only do not need, but you probably should not have and can save money by not having. Remember, now, that what you are now reading was written by a person who makes his living by expressing opinions and suggesting buy and sell ideas. I write a column twice a week in which I suggest possible buys and possible shorts, based entirely on technical considerations and directly related to the ideas expressed within these pages. Yet, if you are going to be a successful trader, the one thing you do not need is someone else's opinion. I believe that the readers of my column (for *RealMoney*, a subservice of TheStreet.com) are primarily looking for ideas. I am a filter, looking at thousands of stocks and whittling the field down to manageable proportions. I hope that those who read my words are then studying the material and making informed decisions, based on the technical picture I have provided but inserting their own judgment. I want to be providing information, rather than opinions. Therefore, I never own the stocks I suggest. I may own others with very similar patterns, but I am not touting a stock because I want the public's help in pushing it in my direction. I will certainly be acting in accordance with the market opinions that I state in my column, but there is no way that such an opinion can be self-serving.

Every day I receive a number of e-mails and many faxes, all touting stocks that are sure to go up. So do you, I would guess. They all go directly into the trash, without passing go or collecting any of my dollars. Do you think someone wants to help you to make money by telling you about the great stock he has discovered? Is he, too, about to buy it? Of course not. He already owns it and wants a sucker to sell it to!

A close relative of the Internet or fax tout is someone you know. Perhaps you are talking with others at a cocktail party or after a PTA meeting. They tell you about the great stock they think you should buy. Perhaps their intentions are worthy, but always keep in mind that nobody ever thinks that a stock is great and tells you about it because they are about to buy it. Be assured that if they are telling you about it, they already own it. That is not to say that their intentions are dishonest necessarily, but they are certainly biased. They are already in a stock, and they want company; they want validation from someone else. That is not a good reason to buy a stock.

OPINIONS AND INFORMATION

We need to differentiate between opinions and information. Buy information, but avoid opinions. I subscribe to the *Wall Street Journal*, and have for close to half a century, because it provides me with information. I use it to double-check prices and statistics. I glean indicators from the pages. Yes, I must admit, I like to read some of the columns. I also look at the sections that tell me what has happened in the markets. But that is not to have the writers tell me what is pushing prices; it is to see what they think is pushing prices. There is a big difference. It is also a way of knowing what may be moving that I had not been aware of. I think the *Wall Street Journal* is a worthwhile expense for anyone wanting to be active in markets. But it is still very important to not be swayed by the opinions that are everywhere. The only important opinion, in the final analysis, is your own. That opinion is what will prompt you to buy or sell a certain stock and to have a particular outlook for the direction of prices in general. The danger is that there will be such an overwhelming consensus that you will be unable to make an unemotional decision. Remember that almost everyone is a bull at the tops of markets, and almost everyone is a bear at the bottoms of markets. There are times when you must be able to shield yourself from the irrational stampede, and go alone in the other direction.

Most other publications are probably unnecessary. *Barron's* will provide you with a great number of statistics that you may want to follow; but it will also provide you with a deluge of opinions that may be harmful. Most advisory letters will give you advice you do not want or need, but they may point you in the direction of stocks you had not thought about before.

CHARTING SERVICES

What you really will need more than anything is a way of reducing the information to a manageable level. In other words, you need charts of the stocks and charts of your indicators. The lines of statistics in the *Wall Street Journal* are no substitute for a picture of what the price and volume have been over time. You can still draw your own charts, of course. It is good training to do so, as it makes each move much more apparent. However, it is time-consuming and carries the danger of you becoming a chart keeper rather than a chart reader. It also limits dramatically the number of issues that can be perused. With the wonderful array of computer products available to today's trader, I believe that not taking advantage of the technology is to assume a handicap. At least on a trading basis, the market is a zero-sum game. For every dollar gained by one person, a dollar is lost by another person. The factors that determine which group you will fall into may be very small and very critical. It does not make sense to reduce your competitive position by ignoring any technological tool that can help you to make better or more rapid decisions.

Provided with this book is a trial CD for the MetaStock charting service. It delivers a month of free access to MetaStock's entire universe of data and its complete charting system, Equivolume being only a small part of it. I suggest using it as you study this book, and then deciding, at the end of the month, whether to continue to use it or to subscribe to another service. In today's markets, in order to remain competitive, I think you must have some charting service. If you currently are subscribing to another service, ascertain if it contains Equivolume charts, and if not, push that service to update. I still suggest, though, that you take advantage of the free MetaStock charts provided, at least during the learning phase, since they conform to the examples used throughout this book.

That is, perhaps, it. Your situation may be such that you want to do your charting and decision making only in the evening, after the markets are closed. If so, all you need is the closing data and the ability to turn it into pictures. From there on it is merely a question of learning to correctly interpret that picture and developing a procedure to act upon the information. Perhaps you will enter orders with limits while the market is closed. If so, you will not even need a quotation source during the trading day. If, however, you wish to watch more closely and perhaps act during the trading day, you will need to have a little more information. With online trading, the company that handles your account will also provide you with up-to-the-minute quotes. You will be able to see the last sale, the bid and asked, the size of the market on both sides, and the volume. Most such sites also give you access to a great number of technical and fundamental tools.

QUOTATION SERVICES

If you are going to follow a large number of stocks, want up-to-date information, and wish to be aware of every tick, you may need to subscribe to a quotation service. There are many out there, and they all provide a great deal of other information. I use the eSignal service. With it I can, if I wish, access a large variety of intraday data. For example, the short-term charts at the beginning of Chapter 7 were produced using this service. Having an intraday quotation service will mean that you can get very close to the market.

This can sometimes be a curse rather than a blessing, however. If you have a tendency to make emotional, and sometimes irrational, decisions, perhaps not allowing yourself to see every tick is a good idea. Placing well-thought-out orders when the markets are closed may be a help in overcoming such a trait. Of course, staying close to markets but obeying your discipline can be advantageous. If, for example, you have decided a certain stock would be a buy if and when it breaks through a certain level with better volume, you can be watching and act as the event occurs. A stop order might do the same thing with regard to price level, but there is no way you can make the stop order contingent upon the volume characteristics of the price change. Being right on top of the action can allow you to inject subtle nuances that would not otherwise be possible. In the final analysis, you need to look at your own personality, your available time, and your interest in becoming intimately involved, and make your own decision.

FINDING A BROKER

Now you are ready to make your decisions, but you are not yet ready to trade. You need a brokerage account. I think the best thing to happen to technical stock traders in many years has been online trading. The reasons are numerous. Perhaps the most important is cost. Commission rates are so low now as to be hardly a factor in making a decision.

The second advantage to online trading is psychological. The worst thing you can do, in my opinion, is to discuss your decisions with someone else. Doing so puts you immediately in a defensive position. You are going to be either right or wrong, and you will have a fear of being wrong and having to justify your decision to the person in whom you have confided. If you make a decision and then do the trade through a broker, perhaps someone who is also a friend or neighbor, your judgment is already compromised and you have a need to be right. There is never a need to justify your actions to a computer. The uninvolved passiveness of the computer-placed trade makes the decisions less emotional. To the fundamentalist, having justifiable reasons—a story—for a trade is sometimes psychologically important. To the technician the story should never be important. The online trade allows detached and unemotional decisions.

The third advantage to an online trade is instant information. Often the report of the trade comes back so quickly that it is there before you have time to click to another screen. That sets the stage for immediately setting a protective stop. Also, there is less reluctance to place a large number of orders that never get executed. If you are using a strategy of placing stop orders to initiate new positions, you will place many orders each day that never get done and expire at the end of the day. Your busy broker, trying to make a living by talking to as many people as possible each day, would find all those orders with so few trades to be an irritant. The computer does not care. Neither should you.

If you are putting together a long-term income portfolio to see Aunt Maude through her declining years, perhaps a live broker can help you. I am not denigrating good financial planning. But that is not the aim of the trading we are discussing here. For our objectives, I believe online trading is the best way to go. The one thing you do not want is someone else's advice, so why pay for it?

Another advantage we have gained because of technology has been decimalization of prices. The switch from eighths and quarters to cents per share has made it possible to take advantage of the small moves that the low commissions have made profitable. The flow of prices is now smoother. The smallest changes in attitude are now apparent. Limits can be placed closer to critical levels. Instead of having a stop executed by an eighth of a point move, it can be touched off by a move of just a cent or two.

A large number of good online brokers are available to choose from. You will want a margin account, as we have discussed elsewhere, in order to be able to go long or short. To not do so would not only limit you to only the buy side of the market, but it would tend to bias you to a bullish position, since you would want to trade, not sit out a down market. However, you will find that you are not allowed to have a margin account in a retirement account. To get around that problem, I keep two accounts. One is a tax-sheltered individual retirement account (IRA), and the other is a regular margin account. Then I do my long trades in the retirement account and do my shorts in the margin account. This system allows me to remain market neutral if I wish or place emphasis on the side of the market that appears to be dominant at any particular time.

Opening an account is usually quite quick and easy. Next you need to get familiar with the mechanics of using the site for placing trades, for seeing where you are, for monitoring your current positions, and for determining profits and losses. The competition between online brokers has become so intense that there is a plethora of information and help available to you, regardless of which broker you select.

HOW MUCH MONEY?

The next question is always, "How much money should I have in order to use this methodology?" There is, of course, no set answer. It depends on the resources of the individual, the temperament of the individual, and the goals and needs of the individual. Certainly it should not be all of a person's resources. Trading is an aggressive technique. Also, it should not be the grocery money. It must be money that can be set aside and not depended on for other needs. Ideally it is only a part of a well-planned financial blueprint, determined by the needs and resources of the individual. A good financial planner can be helpful in making such a determination. But remember what we were saying earlier; the financial planner may help you to decide how much money to earmark for trading, but the actual trading should be up to you.

You should be able to trade a few positions at a time, and you should be able to trade reasonable-sized pieces in order to minimize the effect of the cost of buying and selling. But that does not mean thousands of shares. Perhaps the ability to trade a hundred or more shares at a time in a half dozen medium-priced stocks, and to do so without worrying if it will affect your ability to pay the rent or mortgage, is a reasonable minimum level. Beyond that, the most important limit to the upside is going to be determined by how well you handle stress. Buying and selling stocks, and watching them go with you or against you, is an emotional, often traumatic, experience. It should not unduly influence the rest of your life. If you are losing sleep over your trades, you are trading beyond your emotional means. Ideally, one should be able to remain quite detached and businesslike in order to not make bad decisions. A trader I once knew used to say, "We only use money to keep score."

With all of these details in place, the final preparation is to decide what time frame you are interested in using for your trading. Do you want to be a day trader, or do you want to hold positions for many months? The decision will be based on your resources, both of money and of time, and your emotional makeup.

CHAPTER 7

Choosing Your Route

How far is it from Chicago to New York? About 700 miles, right? Sure, if you are flying directly from O'Hare to La Guardia. But what if you are driving, and decide you want to stop and see an old high school friend in Cleveland and a recent acquaintance in Philadelphia? Now it is a bit longer trip. Or suppose instead that you want to stop at every large city within 50 miles one side or the other of the direct route. Then you will make a great number of back-and-forth jogs on your way to New York. Suddenly the distance from Chicago to New York has become far longer. If you want to stop and walk up to the front door of each house along the way it will become really long. The distance from Chicago to New York can be infinitely long, if you plan it that way.

In trading stocks we need to decide not only where we are going but also how circuitous a route we are going to take. How far are we going to be willing to stray from the intended path? Are we going to wander along the country byways, or arrow over the interstates? Are we going to be willing to get lost and have to backtrack from time to time, or are we going to worry every time the road seems to be swinging away from a direct line to our destination?

THE FRACTAL MARKET

It is amazing to note that stock charts, even Equivolume charts, are fractal. This term, borrowed from chaos theory, merely means that it does not matter what time frame we are looking at—the picture looks very much the same. A weekly chart has formations similar to those on a daily chart, and the formations on a daily chart resemble those on an hourly chart. As long as it's an active enough item being charted, even a one-minute chart looks very similar to a much longer-term chart—so much so that if we were looking at a chart of an active issue, with no time frame defined, it would be difficult to guess whether it was an hourly chart or a daily chart.

We find, therefore, that every small formation becomes a part of a larger formation, and every large formation consists of a number of smaller ones. A flag on a one-minute chart might last for only five entries (i.e., five minutes), so it becomes just a single entry on the five-minute chart. A wedge might last 10 entries on the hourly chart, but disappear on the daily chart. On a weekly chart we would be unaware of the smaller hourly moves that contributed to the entries. Yet these smaller chart shapes are useful if you are trading in that time frame. As we go through typical consolidations and their interpretation we will be looking at daily charts, but remember that the same patterns are available to you if you have the technological ability and the data flow to look at intraday real-time data.

What makes the fractal nature of markets important to us is that we can take advantage of any of the time frames, and apply the same rules and observations. As long-term investors we can be looking at a large rectangle formed in the Dow Jones Industrial Average over a three-month period, or as short-term traders we can be looking at a flag in IBM over the past two weeks. But at an even smaller level, if we want to be day traders, we can observe the same sorts of wedges, triangles, pennants, and rectangles on charts that have a posting for every five minutes of trading, and apply the same rules. That means that aggressive day traders can use a real-time data feed, similar to Equivolume charts, but posted on a very short-term basis, and take advantage of the tiny intraday market moves.

Particularly noticeable is the similarity in the short-term consolidations. We have flags, pennants, and rectangles in a one-minute chart, with breakouts that have usable measurement characteristics, just as we do in a daily chart.

In Figure 7.1, we are looking at the Dow Industrials on a number of days in 2006–2007. (Figures 7.1 and 7.2 are bar charts rather than Equivolume charts, and are provided by eSignal, Inc., my intraday data source.) Each vertical line in Figure 7.1 represents one hour of trading. Notice how a single day of trading (seven entries) can enclose an entire chart formation like a pennant. Carrying it to the even more diminutive, in Figure 7.2, captured at the same time as the hourly chart, we see a picture of just part of the current trading day, with each entry representing just one minute of trading. Here, too, we have similar patterns, but patterns that had been hidden on the hourly chart. Notice the flag on the way up at about 11:10 that day. It was a typical flag, and it was a resting point just about halfway up the full move. We will, in the following pages, look at very similar examples of price action and very similar measuring techniques, but applied to Equivolume daily charts.

The fractal nature of consolidations gives us an opportunity to look at markets in a way that is different from what has been the traditional way. Usually technicians look

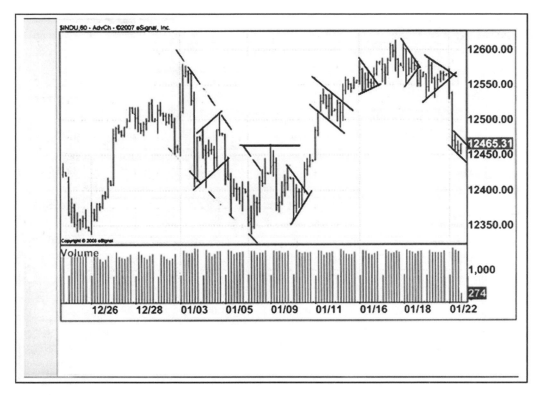

FIGURE 7.1 Hourly Chart of the Dow Industrials. Copyright © 2007 eSignal, Inc.

at charts and identify small and large consolidations. The time limit on the small ones like flags and pennants is usually about three weeks for a normal formation. But perhaps that is only because of the time frame being studied. If, as I have shown, the markets are fractal, then the short-term formations become a part of the larger formations. So, a small flag on a five-minute chart can be combined on that chart with others near it, and a larger shape, like a triangle, is recognized. But if we then move to a 60-minute (hourly) chart, we find that the combination of consolidations we saw on the short-term chart is crammed into a recognizable single formation—again, a flag, pennant, and so on.

My thought is that instead of trying to identify the bigger formations on the chart, we should change the time scale and see what is forming at a different level. This approach would have been difficult or impossible at the time when all charts were hand drawn, but now, with computers, it is so easy to move from time frame to time frame that it is simpler and perhaps more accurate to move out to a different time frame rather than try to find new names and new interpretations for the longer-lasting patterns. Perhaps there are only a very few possible patterns, but at different scales of magnification.

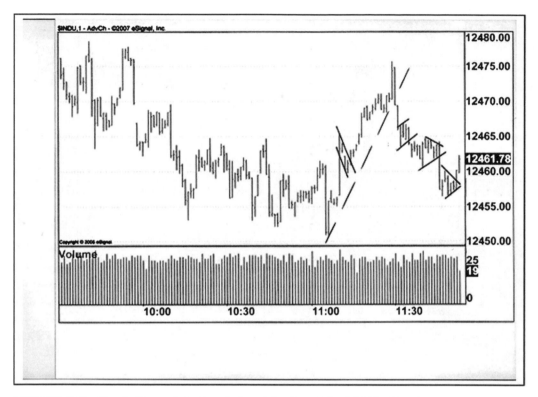

FIGURE 7.2 Hourly Chart of the Dow Industrials. Copyright © 2007 eSignal, Inc.

Figure 7.3 shows a daily chart. On it the various formations, usually lasting a few days to a few weeks, are indicated. They fall into the standard concept of a consolidation and obey the rules well. But then, in Figure 7.4, we have compressed the data so that each Equivolume box represents a week of trading. Suddenly the formations we were looking at on the prior chart have disappeared. But now we have a whole new set of patterns. They, too, are quite uniform in duration, but now it looks as though the typical consolidation lasts three or four months.

VALUE OF RECOGNIZING YOUR TIME FRAME

What, then, is the value to us in recognizing this fractal nature? It means that we can go out to a longer time frame and put the current action into a better perspective. If we are, for example, long a stock that seems to have formed a series of sideways moves, perhaps they actually will blend into a single formation on the longer-term chart. Perhaps by seeing that, we can get a better feel for the longer-term direction of the stock.

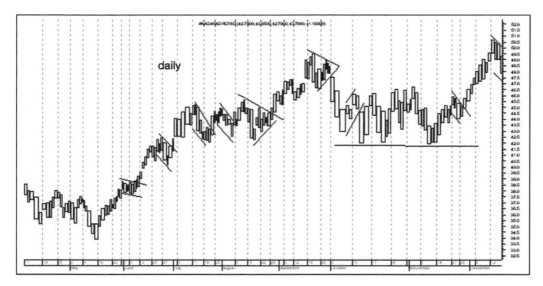

FIGURE 7.3 Daily Chart of Anadarko Petroleum.

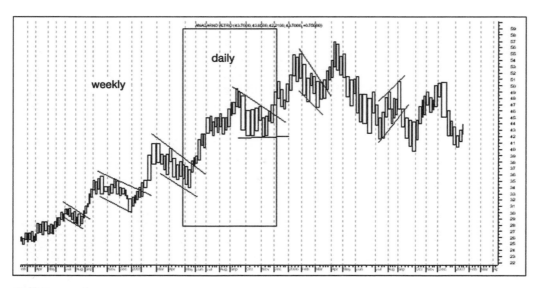

FIGURE 7.4 Weekly Chart of Anadarko Petroleum.

"So how have you been doing in the market, Gary?" I asked.

"Not so good. I bought W. R. Grace exactly a year ago, and I am behind by half a point. That's no big deal on a $10 stock, but not very exciting, either. But I'm in it for the long term."

Figure 7.5 shows the stock Gary was talking about. He had held it from September 2005 to September 2006. He was so sure he was in it for the long term that he had ignored the shorter-term swings. Gary had decided he was a long-term investor, not a short-term trader. He was going to stay on the interstate until he reached his distant intended exit.

At least Gary knew what his time frame was. Sometimes we may be in a stock with the idea that we are longer-term holders, but a short-term gain presents a quick profit we are unable to resist taking. We become short-term traders when we intended to be long-term investors.

At other times we start out thinking we are short-term traders and later, when a position does not work out right, we decide we are long-term holders. A good friend of mine, who has made that excuse to cover an error more times than he would like to admit, jokingly says that his tombstone is going to read, "I'm in it for the long term."

But in the previous example, there could have been some extremely good profits realized by knowing, in advance, what sort of a trader one was, and looking for those changes of direction that fit those intentions. On these examples I have used a line chart, so that the pattern is smooth and discernible.

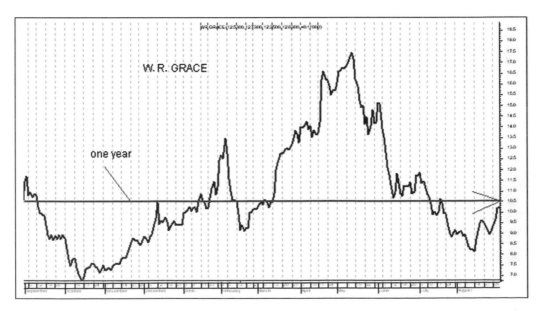

FIGURE 7.5   One Year of W. R. Grace.

It is not difficult to see that there were a number of large and lasting moves in the stock during the year in which Gary about broke even. In Figure 7.6, I have drawn arrows through the patterns and numbered them. There are three advances and three declines. Let us make the optimistic assumption that we are able to buy and sell quite near each of the turning points. The three up moves would have produced a total profit of about 19 points. On a $10 stock, in one year that is a pretty good gain. If Gary were only to go short on the declines and have the same good timing as we have earlier assumed, the gain would be about 17 points. So, if he had been willing to try to capture both the up moves and the down moves, he might have garnered about 36 points ($36) on a $10 stock in one year. Wow! And in only six trades.

It is obvious that, in this case at least, playing the major waves was much more profitable than just holding and forgetting. But if that strategy pays off, maybe it would be possible to trade the even smaller wave patterns and make even more money. Each of the waves has a smaller pattern of ups and downs.

The next smaller wave pattern is shown in Figure 7.7. Each of the larger waves is interrupted by one or more counter moves, with the exception of the sharp decline that is leg 7. The result is 20 up or down legs, rather than the six of the larger pattern. Again, if we assume we catch each of those moves, and we get in and out in a timely manner, capturing most of each swing, the results are spectacular, but of course unrealistic to expect. There are 10 up positions and 10 down positions. The buys produce a profit of

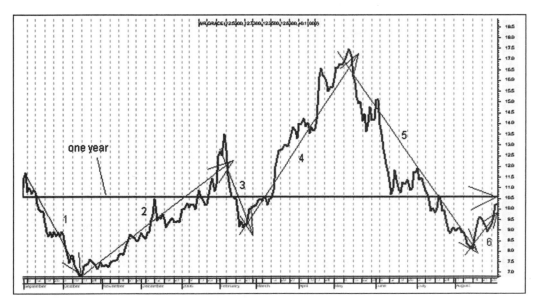

FIGURE 7.6 The Major Waves in W. R. Grace.

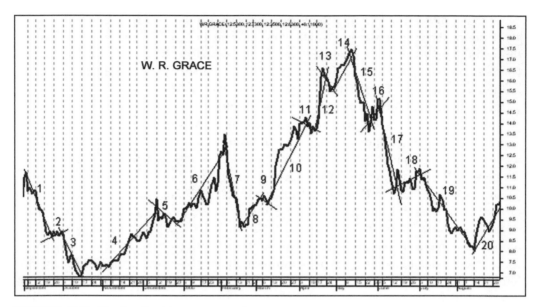

FIGURE 7.7 The Smaller Waves in W. R. Grace.

18 points, and the shorts produce a profit of 19.25 points. That is a total of $37.25 for the year, compared to $36 in the earlier calculation. On a $10 stock, that is good. But there are a great many more trades, and therefore a great deal more is paid in commissions and a great deal more work is done making the decisions. Moreover, the shorter-term swings would have been less easily identified.

Let's take this comparison a step further. In Figure 7.8, we are looking at just the last part of the prior chart, and we are looking at a bar chart in order to have more details. Legs 19 and 20 consist of eight smaller swings, with each up or down leg having a duration of just a few days. Again, we are going to be taking a more circuitous route to our destination and covering even more ground. That means bigger possible profits, but also bigger commissions to be paid and a great deal more analytical work to be done.

Of course, it is even possible to narrow the time frame far more, until one becomes a day trader. The trade count skyrockets, and the commissions do likewise, but the results can be spectacular if you are able to be right much of the time. For those with the time, nerves, inclination, and ability, the methods I am presenting in this book have their application in the various time frames, even day trading. It is interesting to note that Equivolume charts plotted on a 5- or 10-minute basis usually obey the same rules as those in play on daily charts.

The consideration is, then, how much work you want to do in order to take advantage of smaller and shorter-term wave patterns. And in addition, you must realize that

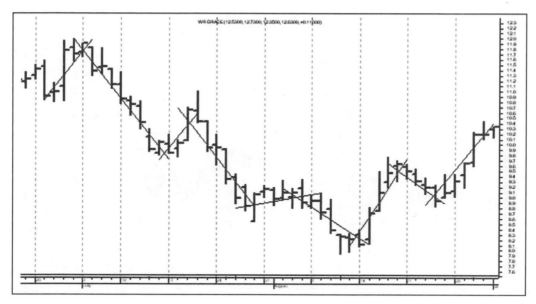

FIGURE 7.8 The Ripples in W. R. Grace.

interpretation gets more difficult and action becomes less predictable as one moves to a shorter-term wave pattern. In this book we are primarily looking at the waves that tend to last only weeks, rather than the long-term holds. But we are avoiding getting down to the smaller waves. Keep in mind that the direction of the wave pattern you are trading is going to be signaled by the next smaller wave pattern. Therefore, you will always be looking at the time frame that is one size smaller than the one where your money is.

Any trading that involves holding stocks for more than a day, but is based on market action rather than fundamentals, is generally referred to as swing trading. Even if you are a swing trader, you need to decide which wave pattern you are going to try to capture. That means studying and classifying the action on the stock you are thinking of using before initiating a trade, and realizing the types of waves the stock is likely to generate. For most traders I believe it is most advantageous to try to capture the waves that last a number of weeks or months and to try to avoid becoming too short-term by moving with each ripple. In other words, on the W. R. Grace stock, it would be best to try to capture the three up and/or the three down moves in the year, rather than trying to make the small additional profits that might be possible by trading the 20 smaller waves. But that is not always easy. Your own fear and greed are constantly trying to move you to shorter time frames.

Some stocks make it look easy because the trends are so easily discerned, such as Fannie Mae in 2006, shown in Figure 7.9. On this chart, each move is well defined and

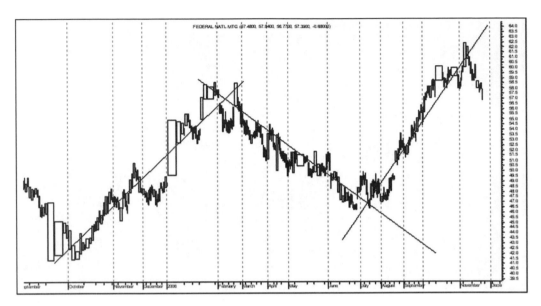

FIGURE 7.9   Major Trends in Fannie Mae.

well signaled. More important is the lack of counter moves that might have been mislead-ing. This stock would have made staying with the position for the full move quite easy. Unfortunately, that is not always the case.

For example, in the same time frame we have Boeing, shown in Figure 7.10. The swings were very similar, but the two countertrend moves, enclosed in ellipses, would have been very hard to ignore, and doing so would have resulted in leaving a great deal of profit on the table. It is this sort of activity that turns a longer-term swing trader into a short-term trader.

So the first consideration in knowing which time frame to trade is a personal deci-sion. It is based on how much time and work you are able or willing to do. Earlier in this chapter we looked at the fractal nature of the markets and realized that there are many time frames that can be profitable. But they can be profitable only if they are used correctly. How they are used is dependent upon the time and effort expended. So, decide whether you want to buy stocks to hold them for the longer moves lasting months or you want to watch each swing and try to take advantage of the swings that last a few days or weeks. Be sure you define this to yourself and stay with it. The real world of trading has a way of twisting well-thought-out intentions. If you have bought a stock because it has a well-defined pattern of swings up and down lasting a number of months each, do not get out as soon as you have small profit. Remember your time frame. Perhaps no other tool is so helpful in this regard as the use of stop orders, which we discuss extensively in Chap-ters 10 and 11. If properly placed, they allow us to walk away from a position and not be

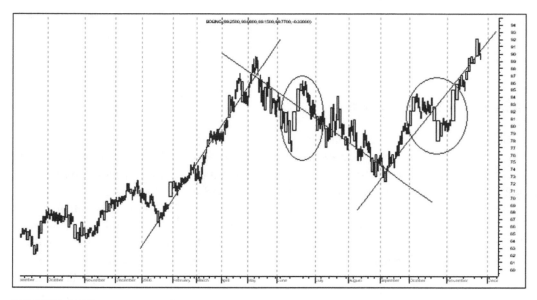

FIGURE 7.10 Countertrend Moves in Boeing.

worried or tempted. The beauty of the method is that the stops are placed objectively, before we are influenced by subsequent up or down swings. They remove the danger of making an emotional decision. The trick is to place the stops in accordance with our time frame decision. Buying a stock to take advantage of the longer-term moves, but then placing a stop so close that we are taken out by a minor wiggle, is not productive.

KNOWING YOURSELF

The next consideration is closely related to the first. It entails the correct evaluation of our own temperament. Having all the necessary time and access to all the available information to allow us to be day traders does not mean that we are of the temperament to be day traders. Having a great deal of information at one's fingertips, literally in today's keyboard age, can be a detriment at times. It magnifies every small swing in our minds. We see that we are up hundreds of dollars in a position in just a day or two, and are powerfully tempted to take the profit. Or, conversely, we see a small loss and are afraid it will get bigger, so we jump back out. The opposite danger is, having decided to be short-term traders, letting a position convert us to being longer-term holders through wishful thinking. In both these cases the use of stops is a great help. Basically, it is necessary for each of us to decide what type of market activity suits our temperament and our access to information. In general, I believe the tendency is for the trader to become impatient and shorten the time horizon, and yet it is usually better to develop more patience. Without meaning to, we tend to shorten the time frame, whereas, if properly done, it is usually advantageous to lengthen on the time frame.

KNOWING YOUR STOCKS

The third consideration is the nature of the stock being used as a trading vehicle. Either you will need to find stocks that suit your time frame or you will have to alter your actions to suit the rhythm of the stock being traded. Remember that each stock is an individual with its own characteristics. You need to be in sync with that rhythm.

On the chart of Enbridge Energy (Figure 7.11), we see a quite regular cyclicality. The stock price appears to go up for two months and then down for two months. Actually, the cyclicality is based on volume, as we will see in Chapter 18's discussion of volume cycles. On an Equivolume chart, since the x-axis represents volume, the regularity becomes very apparent. Obviously, then, this stock is suitable for someone who is trying to trade on an intermediate-term basis. Each of those up and down cycles represents a good opportunity for a substantial profit. It is worthwhile to go through the exercise of putting in lines to generalize the swings, as has been done on the Enbridge Energy chart. These trend lines define the rhythm of the stock. We need to either find stocks that suit our rhythm or change our thinking on each issue to take the rhythm into consideration. That means an initial step of recognizing the rhythm.

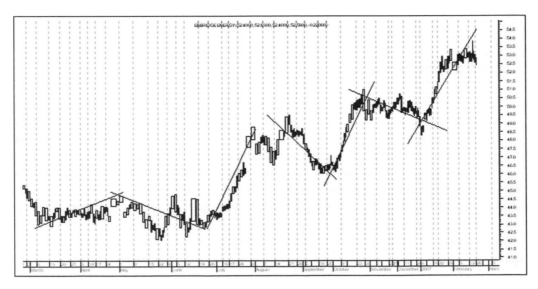

FIGURE 7.11 Enbridge Energy.

Compare that to the chart of Microsoft (Figure 7.12), where there are fewer and longer cycles. Looking for a two-month cycle such as we saw in Enbridge Energy would mean leaving a great deal of money on the table.

But never forget that a stock can change its rhythm. A stock that has been going through a series of short-term swings can suddenly go into a steady advance or decline. Perhaps the best profits over the years have come when I have been in a stock that changed its characteristics. In fact, when we are looking for a power box as a signal to go into a stock, we are looking for a change in personality for a stock. The regular cycles can produce regular and respectable gains, but the changes in stock personality can lead to the really big plays. There is the danger that we may get out of a stock with a small gains because it looks as though it has finished a cycle, and thereby miss the less common but big moves. Again, it is the stop order that is the best way to guard against this. If you never get out of a situation with a market order, you are never predicting a turn. You are admitting that the stock is always right, and you are willing to let it tell you its story.

To summarize: There are a number of considerations in choosing the route you wish to travel. Are you going to day trade? Are you going to try to take advantage of every little day-to-day swing? Are you going to watch each larger swing, but be unwilling to take a small profit or loss? Or are you going to buy a group of stocks, put in stops, and go on vacation? First you need to define your own aims, resources, and time constraints. The extent of the electronic services and computer power you have available may dictate which approach you use. The amount of work you are willing to do will certainly be a

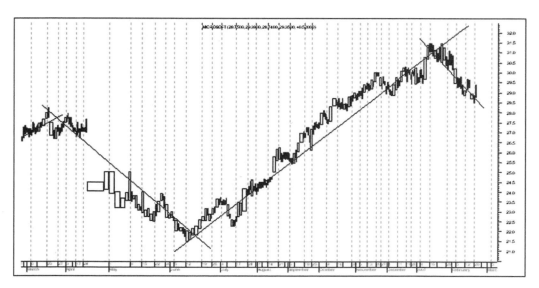

FIGURE 7.12 Microsoft.

factor. The risk you want to assume and the excitement you want to generate are also factors. Most important, perhaps, is the amount of money you have available, and what part it plays in your financial situation.

But the biggest consideration is your own temperament. How much pressure can you take, and how much pressure do you want to take on? Can you be completely objective in your decisions, or are you going to cave in to your emotions? Are you willing to sit out unfavorable markets? Are you willing to take a position when the consensus of the street says you are wrong? You must decide whether you have the temperament to be a day trader or an aggressive swing trader. If so, the methods we are looking at will make your short-term trading much less traumatic. But you still must be in control of your natural fear and greed, and you must stick by a plan.

The next step is to find stocks that meet the requirements you have established, and the spectrum is very wide. In the next chapter we take a look at just how wide that spectrum is.

The next step is finding stocks that can lead to profits. Often a stock acts in such an unusual manner that it immediately comes to the attention of an observant technician. Volume and price movement combine to produce what we call a power box. In the next chapter we will look at these power boxes, and how they can be recognized and capitalized upon.

CHAPTER 8

Power Boxes

No Equivolume signal is more important than the power box. It should be the foundation of your trading strategy. A power box on a stock chart is much like a bright red Ferrari Testarossa taking off from a stoplight. After a period of idling quietly it suddenly leaps forward. A great deal of horsepower comes into play as it accelerates. In just a few seconds it has covered a rather large distance, making enough noise to draw everyone's attention. The impression is that a powerful force has suddenly been let loose.

Figure 8.1 shows AutoZone in late 2006. Leading up to the box marked as a power box, the stock had been moving sideways, idling at the light. It had edged forward and then rolled back a number of times, always stopping its advance right at the edge of the intersection. I have marked the crosswalk as the resistance line. But suddenly the light changed, the driver stepped on the gas, and the Ferrari lunged forward through the intersection and up the highway. After that we saw a number of times where the driver put in the clutch and shifted gears. Each gear shift is seen as a lighter-volume slowing or deceleration, followed by a new spurt of strength in the next gear range. The result is a number of successive tall and wide Equivolume boxes to the upside as the advance progresses.

The key to getting into the stock early in the move was the power box. It told us that something had changed. We did not know, or even care, why it had changed; it was enough just to know we were dealing with a different situation. Undoubtedly there was a reason for the sudden advance. It might have been a public disclosure, or it could just as easily have been something the public would never hear about, or would hear about later. I like to see whether there is news, not because I am looking for reinforcement, but

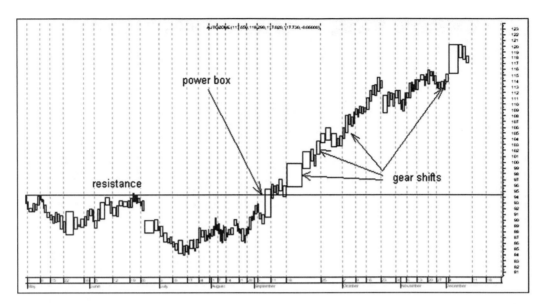

FIGURE 8.1 AutoZone, Late 2006.

just to know if the public will have something to blame the sudden change in attitude on. Often the best moves are the inexplicable moves.

TYPES OF POWER BOXES

Power boxes come in various ways. The first chart was a move out of a sideways consolidation. Figure 8.2 shows the same stock one year earlier, when it started another advance. In this case, though, it went almost directly from a downtrend to an uptrend. To return to our analogy of the Ferrari, it looks as though, instead of stopping at a light, the driver braked for an instant, twisted the steering wheel, and spun the car around enough to be headed in the other direction. From the standpoint of a trader, the first two days on the upside after the turn were on light trading, not telling us enough to prompt a buy. But the acceleration the next day, with heavy volume and a widening trading range, produced an unmistakable power box. The power was so sudden that a gap was left behind. We call that a breakaway gap.

The message seemed to be that we were seeing a dramatic turn to the upside in the stock. From there, as in the prior example, there were a number of hesitations, which I like to call gear changes or shifts. The key, though, was that volume continued to come in on the up days and dry up on the pullback days. We had a series of higher highs and higher lows as the uptrend continued.

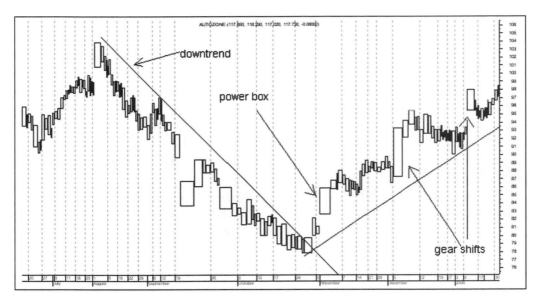

FIGURE 8.2 AutoZone, Late 2005.

In this case, a turn-on-a-dime reversal was very successful. But one has to be more cautious with this type of power box, because at the time of the reversal there was little cause for a lasting effect. The wider a base, the better the subsequent advance is likely to be. In this case there was no real base until the first gear shift. At that time one might say that the entire preceding two months was a base, and that the box I have labeled as the first gear shift was actually the telling power box.

For a box to be classified as a power box it is not enough that we see a big increase in volume and trading range. The second requirement is that either a resistance level or a trend line must be decisively penetrated on the move. Without that we do not have a confirmation of a change of direction. The power box has to overcome a problem in order to have significance. One of the jobs of the trader is to try to ascertain the importance of the level or trend line being penetrated.

NOT ALL BIG BOXES ARE POWER BOXES

Not every big and wide box that breaks though a resistance level is a power box, however. It is very important that the big box come in at or after a change in direction, not late in a move. We have seen a number of other days that also looked like power boxes, but they were much later in the advance so we called them gear shifts. Probably the best rule of thumb is to label a box as a power box only if it is the *first* heavy-volume box with a big trading range in the opposite direction from what has been the norm. In the case of a buy rather than a short (which we will look at in a few pages), that means that the preceding boxes have tended to trade heavier volume to the downside and light volume on rallies right up until the sudden power box to the upside occurred.

In Figure 8.3, Macrovision in 2005 and 2006, we see the difference between big boxes and a particular type of big box: the power box. The first big box is a new development, compared to what has gone before. For the first time, volume has come in on the upside rather than the downside. Second, the stock has broken through a key resistance level. Third, it was so strong it even left a breakaway gap in its wake. The entry was both wide and tall, indicating a burst of energy.

Now look at the next big box. Again, it has moved well in terms of volume and range, and it has gone through the prior highs. This is not the first time a big box has happened, so it seems to be a confirmation of the up move, but a somewhat late time to become a buyer. The next big box is strong, but is not going through any particular level. It is just a continuation of the move. Finally we have the very large box at the top of the move. It, too, leaves behind a gap. The problem is that it is now so late in the advance that the heavy volume may actually be the start of liquidation rather than the start of accumulation that we saw five months earlier. This big day is not the penetration of anything we can see, and the gap has to be somewhat suspect so late in an advance. It is not truly classifiable as an exhaustion gap, but neither could it be called a breakaway or a runaway gap. Later, in retrospect, it is shown to have been an exhaustion gap.

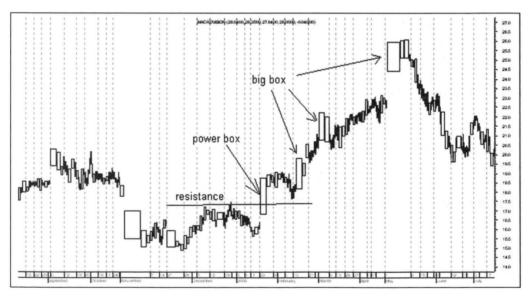

FIGURE 8.3 Macrovision, 2005–2006.

It should be said that all profitable moves do not necessarily start with a power box. For example, a very strong longer-term signal is a saucer top or bottom. In that case there is a gradual change in attitude rather than an abrupt change. But in both cases a change has come into the stock: a change in the supply and demand equilibrium. Also, of course, some apparent power boxes do not lead to the anticipated move. Power boxes are so strong a signal, however, that they should be the most important single factor in looking for either buys or sells.

POWER BOXES ARE COMMON

I suggest that a reader stop at this point and bring up a sampling of charts on his or her computer, using the Equivolume method. Go to a number of different stocks, any stocks, but particularly large "household name" stocks that get a lot of trading, and scroll back in time looking for advances lasting a number of months. Then observe how often those advances are announced at their inception by a power box. It does not have to be the heaviest-volume box on the chart, but it must stand out as a sudden increase in volume. Moreover, it is likely to be the first time in a number of months that the volume has come in heavily on the upside. The big boxes preceding it during the declining phase are usually getting the heaviest volume on the downside. This should make it evident that power boxes are extremely important and that they are easily spotted only using the Equivolume method.

Figure 8.4 gives another example of a power box to the upside. Then afterward we also have a power box to the downside.

First let's look at the advance. The power box to the upside was extremely apparent. Volume was the heaviest in months, and it produced a taller Equivolume box than any preceding it. So there was heavy volume with a substantial advance. But it also had to satisfy the other requirement that it break through a significant level of resistance. That, too, was done. After a short resting phase it moved higher. The huge up box a month later is particularly interesting. Volume was immense, and it left a big gap in its wake. But this was not a power box, because it was not the first big box out of a base. It looked like a powerful advance, but the gap was disconcerting. One had to wonder if we were looking at an exhaustion gap. In fact it was exactly that; it was wider than it was tall, and it came after a small box. It indicated that a big supply of stock was being offered for sale when the price reached that level. For the next three weeks the stock struggled with the level, but finally overcame the resistance. Had it broken support in that period, and especially if volume and trading range had increased on the downside, there would have been good reason to take the profit and move on.

The strong indication that the up move had not only ended but was being replaced with a down cycle was the power box to the downside. It broke both the uptrend line and

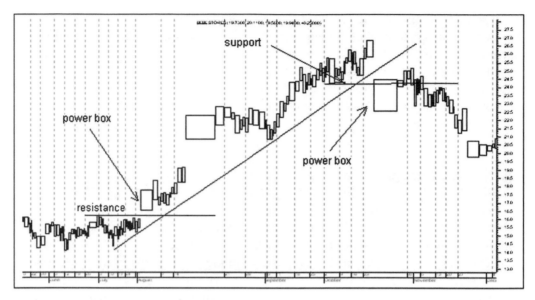

FIGURE 8.4 Power Boxes in Both Directions.

support, and it was the first burst of downside volume. It gapped down, and with enough volume and trading range to suggest it was a breakaway gap in the down direction. After a lighter-volume rally, it went into a large decline. We will talk later about the pullbacks after a power box.

POWER BOXES TO THE DOWNSIDE

Power boxes to the downside, and their volume and movement characteristics, are just the reverse of what we see on the upside, and follow the same general rules. I look for heavy volume with a wide trading range. It needs to be the first such indication of a change in mood. Furthermore, it needs to break a trend line or a support level in a convincing manner to be considered a valid signal. In addition, an encouragement, but not a requirement, is that it will have formed a wide sideways area prior to the break. Just as with a bottom followed by a power box to the upside, I like to see a wide consolidation prior to the move, because it gives a reason for the trend to have legs.

In March 2005, Exxon Mobil made a sharp turn to the downside. (See Figure 8.5.) Volume became the heaviest in months, and the ascending trend line was decisively broken. Prior to that, the volume had been strong on advances, but now we saw a sudden shift in the volume emphasis. The tall and wide Equivolume entry was a clear call to pay attention. After a follow-through the next day there was a rally, but on unimpressive

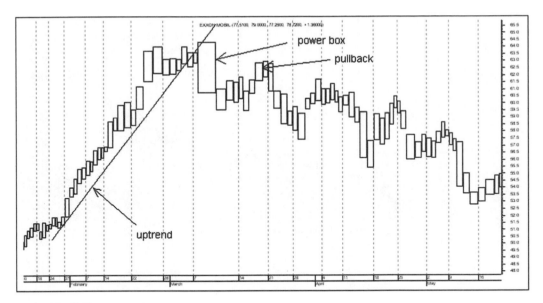

FIGURE 8.5 Downside Power Box.

volume, making the advance suspect. From that point the stock went through almost three months of continuing lower lows, losing about 10 points, or about 16 percent. If we can go back to the Ferrari metaphor, the stock was downshifting as it decelerated.

Does a power box always lead to a substantial move in the indicated direction? Of course not. That is why we need to talk, in other chapters, about stop orders.

There are times when every factor seems to be agreeing with our guidelines, yet the trade does not work out. For example, look at Figure 8.6 of Aquantive in 2005. This stock had been in a well-defined advance. Volume had been coming in on each up move and then drying up on the down moves. Suddenly a big box showed up on the downside, which was made on heavier volume than any day since the advance began three months earlier. It broke the ascending trend line and also dropped through an important support level. After that it even rallied on light volume, and then started to weaken again. It looked like a perfect short. But within days the stock was on the march again.

I do not see any clue here (other than perhaps the bigger down volume on the day about two weeks before the signal day) that could have told us to avoid this situation, yet it was an obvious failure. You will have failures. It is inevitable. When that happens you need to be protected, so that the mistakes are not overly costly. Stop orders can provide that protection.

In this example we took note of the pullback after the downward power box. Had we waited for that pullback before initiating the short position, it would have somewhat mitigated the loss, or even, depending on how we placed our stop, have generated a small

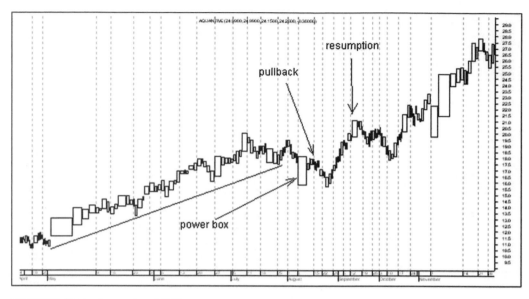

FIGURE 8.6 Aquantive, 2005.

profit on a bad trade. Look back at the prior examples and you will see that in each case there was a lighter-volume move in the days or weeks after the power box that went in the other direction. In all cases shown, it would have enabled entering the position at a slightly better level. Usually, but not always, a power box is followed by a second chance. The power box is formed because of a sudden burst of exuberance on the upside or fear on the downside. Usually that emotion is excessive and leads to second thoughts in the marketplace. Those second thoughts are what we call a pullback. But generally the timidity of the pullback producers is soon replaced by a new burst of activity in the direction indicated by the power box. That means that very often there is going to be a chance to take a position at a better price in the days or weeks that follow the generation of a power box.

It is easy to be caught up on the emotions of the other traders and jump in when the original power box is first generated, but it is dangerous to let our emotions dictate our decisions. Overly bullish action on the part of others should lead to caution rather than participation. If the public is driving a stock too fast, it may be better to let the exuberance run its course, let the second-guessing come in, and then move into the stock. The danger, of course, is that the pullback may never be seen. So you miss a trade. So what? There are lots of other stocks out there. I think it is better to try to use pullbacks for entry points.

Power boxes are the most awesome weapons in your arsenal. They reflect change, and change is what makes money. There are other signals besides power boxes that can help to make a profit, but no others are so reliable, so frequent, and so easily recognized. They can be used either on the long side or on the short side, eliminating being shut out of an adverse market. All stocks do not always give us power boxes on which to act, but there are enough stocks doing so that we need never lack opportunities. It is not difficult to scroll through a long list of stocks on a daily basis, looking for big boxes and thereby identifying power boxes. I use a proprietary computer program that searches through a very large universe of stocks and shows me all those that are producing big boxes. That does not mean that they are all power boxes; most are not. But it is easy to apply the aforementioned rules to classify each big box. The power boxes become obvious. Moreover, it is often possible to spot a big box as it is in the process of formation. Many traders will not want to be watching the market details so closely, but those who do will find that there are times when a big box starts to become apparent during the trading day, allowing entry at a level that is often advantageous. To do so, one must mentally imagine what the final entry for the day is likely to look like, based on what has happened so far.

Power boxes are usually a signal alerting us to the end of a sideways area. Those sideways areas can be continuation patterns, when the stock is just resting, or they can be reversal patterns, indicating a change of direction. Often a consolidation is the precursor to a power box. In the next chapter we look at the interpretation of consolidations.

CHAPTER 9

Okay, Let's Buy

We have found the stock; it has done just what we want. We have seen a big power box after a long decline and a solid base-building period. It even gapped to the upside as it burst through the top of the consolidation. We want to own this stock! But what is the next step? We have a number of choices to make. Do we:

- Act immediately?
- Wait for a lower price?
- Wait for a pullback and renewed strength?
- Wait until it moves higher?

When we do decide it is time to move, do we:

- Place a market order?
- Place a limit order?
- Place a stop order?

Should the order be put in for just the day, or good till canceled (GTC), or some other time frame?

There are no clear answers to all these questions, but some choices are better than others. We want to accomplish a number of things as we go about acquiring the stock. First, we want to get it at an advantageous price. But we do not want to be so cautious about price that we miss the buy entirely. We want to be sure that a better price is not really a sign of weakness, and a reason for not buying rather than buying. We want to have our money in a moving stock, not a dormant stock, so we want to be sure not to get in too soon. We want to be sure the move has legs, but holding back may get us in too late, thereby limiting our profits. We want to be buying a stock because it is strong, which may mean paying up for it. All of these are valid considerations, but often they are conflicting considerations. We need to balance them as we go about our buying.

Let's look at a chart (Figure 9.1). In late August of 2006, General Electric (GE) had been in a consolidation phase for about a month. It was apparent that there was support around the $32 level and resistance around the $33.20 level. This tight trading range is magnified in our very short-term chart, so that we can see the details of the consolidation. After a decline into July there was an attempt to rally the stock, but on the same day it dropped further instead. That led to a gap to the downside the next day. However, beyond the gap the entry was very short and wide—in other words, heavy volume and a narrow trading range. Coming as it did after a decline, it had the characteristics of an exhaustion gap and was the first clue that the decline might be coming to an end. This was interesting, but not a reason to buy. Over the next three weeks GE tested the level twice, with lower volume on each test, suggesting that a possible turn was in the making. Then it suddenly had a very strong day. The trading range expanded and so did the volume. It broke decisively through the descending trend line, indicating a turnaround. Moreover, it went through the top of the area we had identified as the trading range. So it was probably not just going from a downtrend to a sideways trend; it was starting an uptrend. This looked like a move we could call a power box, and was now giving us a reason to want to own the stock . . . but immediately?

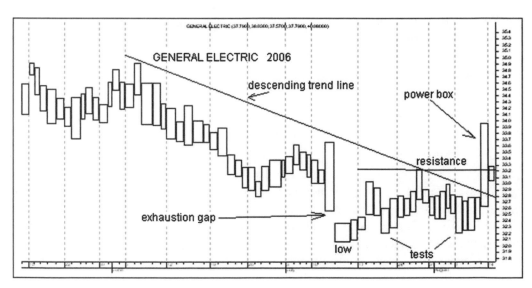

FIGURE 9.1 General Electric, 2006.

If we were watching the market closely and perhaps had computer programs look-ing for volume breakouts, we might have noticed the move above resistance during the breakout day, and if we were very aggressive we might have acted on the breakout. In that case, a market order to buy would have been appropriate, because we would be go-ing with the market, not fighting it, and we would be going into a situation that looked very promising. The stock is of such a liquid issue that we would be able to get an exe-cution right at the current level, so a limit order would not be necessary from that stand-point, either. Waiting carried the danger of having the price move higher before we got in. So, yes, if the buy is going with the direction of the trading, if the stock has plenty of liquidity, and if the move does not look as though it has already progressed too far, a buy at the market order is a good way to go. This assumes, of course, that we are not trading so much stock that we can personally affect the marketplace and force ourselves to pay up too much. Such a consideration is often a function of the liquidity of the stock. In General Electric we would have to be buying a very large block to greatly affect the price. In a thinly traded stock we would have to be much more careful. But if we were a large portfolio manager, a market order would probably not be acceptable. A limit order at or just above the current price would allow our broker to work the stock and acquire it without unduly moving the price.

BUYING THE PULLBACK

But let us assume we are not nimble or informed enough to see the move developing on the breakout day. Certainly, after the market close, the day's power box would practically jump off the page at us as we reviewed our charts. We would want to buy the stock, but be faced with the question of when. The next day there was a slight pullback that would have allowed a buy at a better price. But the question would have arisen as to whether it was just a pullback or the advance was failing. Moreover, by buying on the next day, we would be trying to second-guess the possible extent of a pullback. Also, we would be going against the market direction, rather than with it. I always try to ask myself if am agreeing with or disagreeing with the market. It is always safer to be going with the move. In this case, I think the best stance would be to decide to watch, and buy if the advance resumed. If the pullback wanted to go further, fine. That would also allow us to observe the volume on a pullback, to see if it was lighter trading, as we hoped.

But the next day was very informative, as we see on the extended chart, Figure 9.2. The stock gapped upward with heavier volume and a widening trading range. It had to be interpreted as a strong gap because both the range and the volume increased across the gap. Because it was not going through a prior resistance level, it could not be labeled as a true breakaway gap, but neither was it an exhaustion gap. This was a clear sign of renewed strength, and hinted that the pullback on light volume we were waiting for

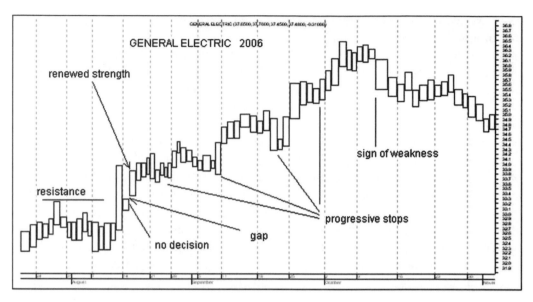

FIGURE 9.2 Progressive Stops in General Electric.

was not coming in. Buying here would mean we were going with the trend and with the volume. Again, a market order seems appropriate.

The ensuing advance is classic. Each up move is followed by a lighter-volume pull-back, stopping at a higher level. That allows the moving up of a stop order. Finally, late in October, there is a down day in which volume increases perceptibly. It is a sign of weakness that suggests the advance has run its course, and that it is time to take the profits.

LIMIT ORDERS AND STOPS

When you enter a limit order you are arguing with the market, but when you enter a stop order you are agreeing with the market. That may sound strange, but consider what you are doing when you put in a limit order to buy a stock. You are placing an order below the current price, so that you will buy the stock if it goes down. But if it is going down, it is going in the wrong direction. You are, in essence, saying that you are smarter than the other traders, in that you know that even though the stock is going down now, it is eventually going to go up. So a limit order to buy is really an attempt to catch the turning point in a stock. But the problem is that trends tend to continue more often than they reverse.

In Figure 9.3, we see the decline in Baxter International in the spring and summer of 2002. One might have been tempted to buy the stock when it appeared to have a heavy-volume washout day after a gap. It found support right at the level where it had turned up back in November of 2001. But just to try to buy it at a cheaper price, we put in a limit buy order at the old support level. The next decline, though, proved to be a resumption of the weakness. We were put into the stock just as it started to break further. In reality, if we had just bought the stock when we thought it was going up and we had a stop-loss order in, that stop would have been at about the level where, instead, we bought the stock. Suddenly we were in the position of holding a rapidly dropping stock. Neither scenario is pretty, and the position was not a very attractive one to start with, but certainly the limit buy was more disastrous.

The exception is the limit order to buy at just about the current price in a stock that is acting well. The limit just makes sure you do not get an unfavorable trade due to the vagaries of the ripples that run through the marketplace. Especially in thinly traded stocks and volatile stocks, a limit buy order makes sense, just as protection. However, a limit order away from the market, referred to earlier, is a statement of arrogance. Moreover, it can be an expensive proclamation. Since a trend is more likely to continue than it is to reverse, the odds of a loss go way up.

The limit order to buy makes much more sense in a lateral market than it does in a declining market. If the stock is in a well-defined sideways move, and there are other indications (volume to the upside, for example) that are convincing enough to suggest

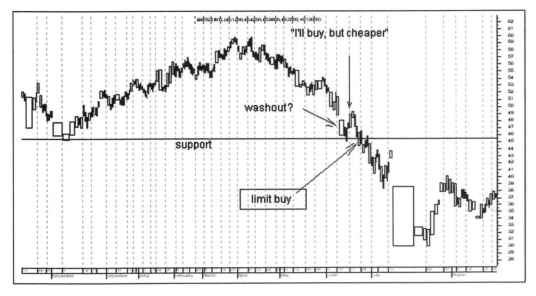

FIGURE 9.3 Baxter International, 2002.

a buy, then a limit to buy, perhaps for a partial position near the bottom of that trading range, is logical. But, of course, a break through the bottom would be a sign the sideways market had become a downtrend, and would call for immediately closing the position.

LATERAL CONSOLIDATIONS

For example, in Figure 9.4 we see Johnson & Johnson's stock in late 2003. The sign of strength was a strong indication the stock was going to go higher. It penetrated the descending trend line with increasing volume and a widening trading range. It also bounced off a level that had repeatedly provided support. At that point we might have decided the stock was entering a sideways area, but with a definite likelihood that it would move out of it to the upside rather than the downside. A buy right after the sign of strength would have meant buying near the top of the implied trading range. A limit order to buy around the low part of the trading range would put us in at a better level. But remember that it is a sideways-trading stock, not a rising stock. Therefore, we are not going with the trend; we are guessing at the probable move.

I would want to have a stop-loss order under the bottom of the trading range, and I would be inclined to put on a partial position rather than buying all I wanted to eventually own. If, for example, I generally put $10,000 into any single position, I would limit my buy to about half that. With the stock at about $50, that would mean buying only 100 shares.

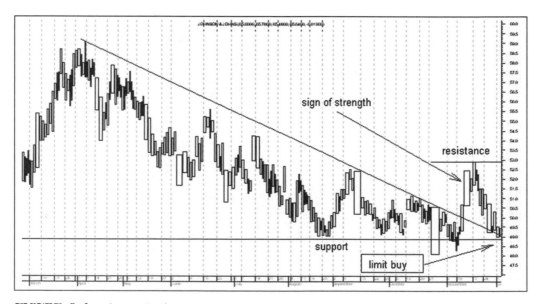

FIGURE 9.4 Johnson & Johnson, 2003.

But the intention would be to watch the position, and if it broke out of the top of the consolidation area, buy the second 100 shares.

Figure 9.5 is a longer-term view of the chart, showing the subsequent action. In this case, at least, the limit buy would have worked out well. The stock did, in fact, move substantially higher, and we would have bought half our stock right at the bottom and the rest on the breakout, producing a good average price.

But generally when we are buying a stock we are buying it because we have seen a power box to the upside develop, indicating the stock is likely to go higher. In that case we are always looking for the pullback as a better buying point. The light-volume pullback after the heavy-volume power box is so likely that I believe we need to try to capitalize on it.

I like to think of the market action, as it comes out of a base, as resembling a football game. (See Figure 9.6.) We have a wide consolidation across the chart, which is not unlike the two teams lined up across from each other at the line of scrimmage. There is often a great deal of pushing and pulling in an attempt to move out of that zone. You have two teams that are evidently quite evenly matched, so that at first neither can gain the upper hand. But then the more aggressive and powerful team manages to penetrate the defense and make a gain or throw the opponents for a loss. It takes extraordinary strength and determination on the part of the successful team to make such a move past the line of scrimmage. So, too, with stocks, it takes a great deal of power to move the price beyond the limits of the consolidation. That power is shown by the heavier volume

FIGURE 9.5 Longer-Term View of Johnson & Johnson.

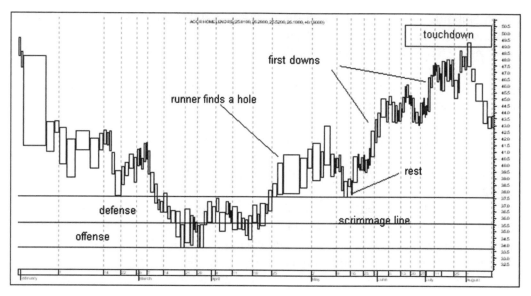

FIGURE 9.6 A Run for the Goal Line.

we usually see on such a move. The penetration that advances the ball and the tackle that puts the team in possession of the ball back both represent a radical change away from the status quo we had been seeing.

To carry the analogy further, I see the breakthrough as either a run or a pass play. The run is a bulling through the resistance on the ground. The ball carrier is forced to traverse every yard of the gain. It takes a great deal of brute power to push the defense aside. In contrast, the pass play leaves a gap behind it. There is a space in which nobody is carrying the ball. This is very much like the power box on our charts that leaves a gap in its wake. Usually the receiver tacks on some extra yardage at the end of the play before he is stopped. That gives us, on our stock, a power box after a breakaway gap.

Usually, after big play, be it a pass or a run, the defense stiffens and tries to push the aggressors back. But if, as the breakout has implied, the defenders are in fact up against a superior force, the only reason they hold is that the opposition is resting and gathering energy for another drive. This is the pullback before the resumption of strength. It is the opportunity we like to look for as a time to buy the stock.

There are times when a stock just continues upward and we are left behind, wishing we had bought it. But more often we do get that pullback, so we need a strategy to best take advantage of it. Carefully placing limit, market, or stop orders can help us to take advantage of a pullback, but to recognize the pullback for what it is necessitates a judgment call. Volume, again, is the key. If the stock starts to move lower after a power box, we want the volume to become lower. If it does, we are being told by the stock that the sellers are not dumping great quantities into the strength. Rather, a smaller number of holders or some smaller holders are taking profits after this first sign of strength. It is normal. It is to be expected. It is usually an opportunity. So, as we trade, we must remain cognizant of the volume. A drop on heavy volume after the power box is likely to be warning to lay off.

Figure 9.7 (of Abbott Labs) shows a very extended pullback, but one with light volume. The difference in possible entry points is very large. If we had bought right after the breakout, we would have been paying around $42 a share. The pullback took the price down to around $39. The problem is in recognizing when the pullback is at its low. I do not think there is any systematic way to do so. In this case we might have been able to see the ascending trend line across the lows, which I have indicated. But that would have been a tough call. Moreover, it would have meant going against that downtrend that had been in effect for about two weeks—in other words, calling a turn when no turn was yet in evidence. Such second-guessing is dangerous.

The approach that I like to use is to buy the stock when it has quit going down in its pullback and has given me a renewed sign of strength. I am willing to pay more than the current price if I am going with the move, rather than against it. So that first day of strength after the pullback is the buy signal. If we are watching closely we will buy it during that day as it starts to move higher after a gap with better volume. The action during that day is a loud call telling us that the pullback is over. We are paying more than the low of the pullback, but are not paying as much as we would have paid two weeks earlier.

FIGURE 9.7 Abbott Labs.

One way to buy a stock in a pullback phase is to place a buy stop order above the top of the downtrend. In this example we might have put in a stop above the original top after the breakout, and then moved it lower as the pullback progressed. That way, when and if the new strength developed, we would immediately and automatically be in. This is an effective method, and one I often use. The advantage is that it gets me in, even if I am not paying attention. The only negative is that there is no volume consideration involved, so I might be going in on a light-volume rally rather than the heavy-volume turnaround I am looking for.

CHAPTER 10

Stop Orders for Getting In

When we decide to buy a stock we have a number of options as to how to buy it. Let us first be sure we all know what the terms mean. In this chapter I refer to these options:

- *Market order.* Buy it for me immediately at the best price you can.
- *Limit order.* Buy it if you can get it at this price or lower.
- *Stop market order to buy.* If it goes up to this price, buy it at the best price you can.
- *Stop limit order to buy.* If it goes up to this price, buy it, but do not pay more than this price for it.
- *Mental stop.* There is no order entered, but I intend to buy it if it goes up to a certain level.

In addition, the orders can be put in for just that day or can be put in to be good till canceled (GTC) or for a specific period such as a month.

The order that is least used is, I believe, the most logical and most effective. That is the stop market order to buy. The stock is at $20. It looks so good on the charts that I want to own it. It has had a power box to the upside that says to me that it is likely to go higher. So I offer to buy the stock, but only if I have to pay more for it! Does this make sense? If it is trading at $20, why would I offer to pay $21 for it? The answer is that I am willing to pay more for a stock that is doing what I want it to do. I am willing to pay up when I am going with the stock, rather than against it. This is the way I prefer to buy a stock, but when I am actually doing so I am always bothered by the action of offering to pay a higher price than the going price. It is a normal feeling that we all experience and have to fight off. It is the thought that I am leaving part of the potential profit behind. Of course, at the same time I am saying that I do not want to own it at all if it does not show me strength.

THE ADVANTAGE OF STOP ORDERS

The beauty of getting into a position by using a stop order is that it tends to keep me out of trouble, it makes me a partner with the market rather than an adversary, and it often saves me money. I am suggesting that there is very little reason to ever buy a stock any other way.

In Chapter 9, we looked at some cases where a market order to buy would have been useful. That was when we were watching very closely and wanted to get in immediately. We also saw that a limit order might be used if it was a thinly traded stock or if we were trying to acquire a large position. But in most cases a stop order to buy would work just as well, and in many cases it would be much better. If it is thinly traded stock, one can use a stop limit rather than a stop market order. That is, once the stop order is touched off by the price moving to the stop level, it becomes a limit order at a price, rather than a market order. If the trade is so big that it cannot be done simply, perhaps a mental stop could be used. But in that case the buyer needs to be very firm in following through on the original plan.

The mental stop allows trading without revealing the size of the intended trade. Even smaller traders may feel more comfortable using a stop limit order rather than a stop market order to avoid getting a big surprise, especially on an opening gap, which sometimes happens. The danger here is that the stock you want to buy never gets bought because the price sails thorough the limit, touches off the stop, and never hesitates long enough to allow the stock to be acquired at your limit price.

I am more inclined just to use a stop market order, so when the price is hit I buy the stock at the best price I can at that time. I prefer the danger of having to pay up to the danger of not owning a stock that is acting well.

THE BUY STOP

First, let's see how a stop order to buy a stock we want to own can get us in at a better level. When a stock gives us a buy signal with a power box, usually we have a resting period before the price goes higher. As we will see in Chapter 15 on flags, pennants, and rectangles, the formation usually takes the shape of downward-sloping small parallelogram that looks like a flag flapping from a flagpole. It can also often be more like a pennant, with lower highs and higher lows. The top of that flag has a downward slope. The important part is that the highs tend to become lower each day for a number of days. The strategy is to put the buy stop order just above that series of downward-sloping highs. That means that as soon as the pattern is violated to the upside the stock is bought. As long as the downtrend continues, the stop price is lowered accordingly, thereby bettering the possible entry level.

Figure 10.1 is a chart of Active Power, which was a low-priced issue that looked as though it had built a base in mid-2005. The big volume advance was an immediate attention getter. After another day of strength, it started to back off on much lighter volume. This looked like a typical pullback. By placing a buy order just above each day's high, as delineated by the top line of the flag formation, the buy order was repeatedly lowered for a week. It took a strong upside day to finally break through the top of the flag formation and touch off the stop buy order. Because of the descending stop strategy, the buy could be done at an advantageous level.

Figure 10.2, a chart of Carmax Circuit City in 2005, shows us a number of flags and pennants. Each one would have given us the opportunity to buy at better levels by not being overly impatient. Descending stop orders would have proved helpful in every case.

There are times, though, when this technique is helpful in another way. It keeps us from ever buying the stock. We want to own a stock only when it is acting strongly. When it is in a pullback it is acting weakly, so we want to hold back until the strength returns. If the strength never returns, we have avoided buying a loser.

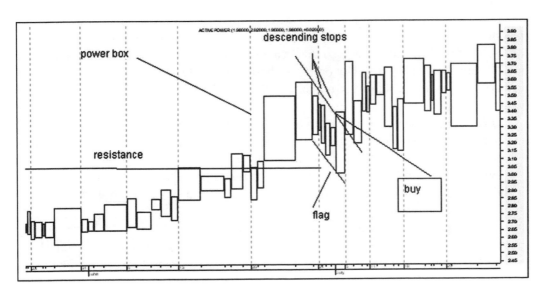

FIGURE 10.1 Descending Stops.

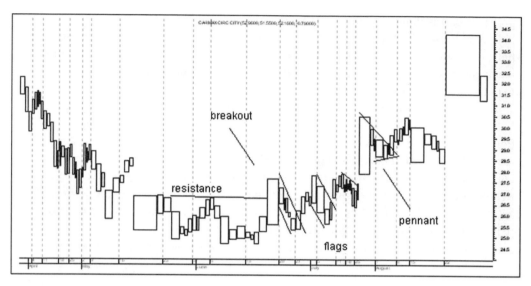

FIGURE 10.2 Flags and Pennants.

I usually like to put in an open stop order rather than a day stop order, and I give the stock a little leeway rather than putting in the stop so close that it gets picked off on a minor fluctuation. Then I look at its location each day, and move it if I think it is necessary. Of course, the stop can only be moved lower, not higher. I am always aware that the stock may decline in such a way, or to such an extent, that I no longer want to own it. If it backs off enough so that it appears to negate the original indication of a buy, I simply cancel the stop buy order. No harm done. If I had simply bought instead of waiting for a renewed sign of strength, I could easily find myself in a stock I no longer want to own.

Anadarko Petroleum looked like a buy to me in September 2006. (See Figure 10.3.) It had built a wide base that had the look of an inverse head and shoulders. It had broken out through the neckline of that structure.

I was tempted to just buy the stock, but instead I put in a buy stop above the high of the subsequent pullback. I decided to keep moving that buy stop order down as the stock declined, if it wanted to.

The decline over the next three days was worrisome. (See Figure 10.4.) I was getting the pullback, but volume was too heavy. There were obviously sellers coming in. However, it was still above the uptrend line. But then, on the fourth day after the power box, we had a gap downward and the ascending trend line was broken. I no longer wanted to own the stock. It was acting wrong, so I canceled the stop buy order. No harm, no foul.

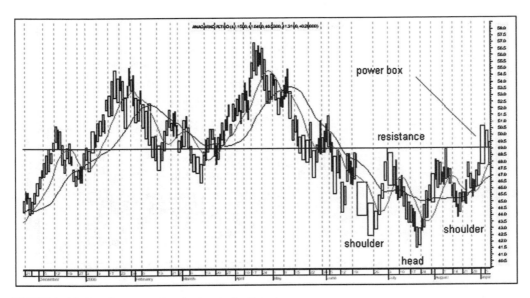

FIGURE 10.3 The Power Box in Anadarko Petroleum.

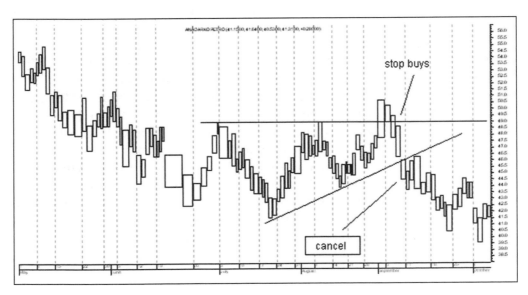

FIGURE 10.4 The Pullback That Went Too Far.

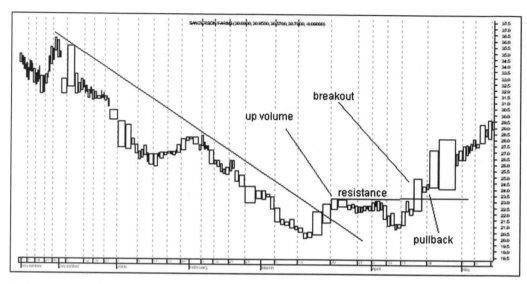

FIGURE 10.5 Sanderson Farms.

Even if the stop order does not get you an appreciably lower price on your buy, it still makes sure you are going with the move, not against it. In April 2006, Sanderson Farms' stock was looking very interesting. (See Figure 10.5.) It had been through a protracted slide since the first of the year. But then it had reversed direction in March with upside volume. This followed months of trading in which volume tended to get heavier on declines and dry up on rallies, so it was starting to act better in mid-March. For a month it moved sideways with lighter trading. But then it suddenly pushed sharply higher with increasing volume and a widening trading range. It penetrated the top of the sideways area it had been in and looked as though it was on its way. The next day it pulled back a little. By putting a stop buy just above the top of the pullback entry, we made sure any upsurge would put us in the stock. After a second low-volume day, the strength returned and the stop level was penetrated. What formed was really more of a rectangle than a flag. In this case there was very little to be gained in terms of price by using a stop buy order, but it did ensure getting into the stock before it ran away. Moreover, if the stock had backed off further or if the breakout was a false signal, the stock would not have been bought.

THE SELL STOP

We have spoken exclusively of buys for the sake of illustration. However, the same techniques are just as effective in putting on a short position. After a sign of weakness such

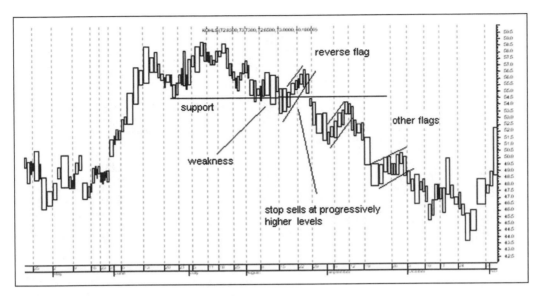

FIGURE 10.6 Shorting with a Stop Order.

as a power box to the downside, a partial retracement on lighter volume is common. It usually takes the form or a flag, pennant, or rectangle. Figure 10.6 shows Kohl's in 2005.

OTHER SIGNALS

Of course there are other reasons than a power box that may lead to buying a stock or selling it short. In those cases, also, a stop order can be very effective. For example, suppose we had been watching the market action in Boston Edison in the second half of 2005. (See Figure 10.7.)

We would have been aware that the uptrend line had been violated and that the stock was moving sideways. In August the down move with heavy volume would have made us pay attention, since it was saying that downward pressure appeared to be materializing. By then we would have noticed that it was looking like a head and shoulders, and we would have drawn in the neckline. After the next rally, what formed looked like the right shoulder; we could then have put in a stop order to go short just below the neckline. A break of that level would have suggested that the decline was starting. The stop would have gotten us in at a good level, automatically.

In the next chapter we are going to look at the more common use of stop orders, as protection once a stock has been bought or it has been sold short. The use of stop orders

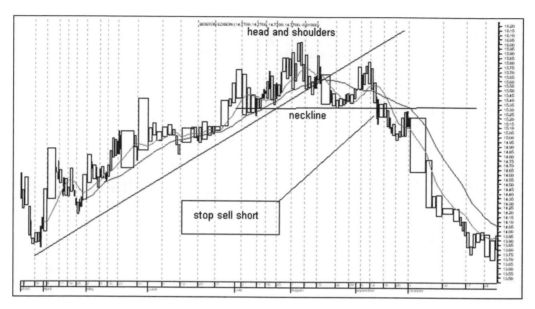

FIGURE 10.7   Head and Shoulders Top.

to get in is as useful a tool, but one that is rarely used by most traders. It can help to get you a better price on your entries; it can keep you from going in on a stock that fails after a breakout; and, most important, it makes sure you are only going with the market, never against it, and never trying to second-guess a turning point.

CHAPTER 11

Stop Orders for Getting Out

As soon as we own a stock or have shorted a stock, we need to be thinking about where we want to or have to get out. That is, we want to if it goes with us, and have to if it goes against us. I believe there is only rarely any reason to get out of a stock using any method except a stop order. By following that regimen we are conforming to our thesis that the market is always right, and we are just trying to go along with it. The rare exceptions might be when we are looking at such an extreme situation, and such a compelling chart pattern, that sitting around waiting to give it back makes no sense. That would most likely be seen if a stock suddenly formed a gap and then traded in very heavy volume in a very narrow trading range. It would look like an exhaustion gap, as described in Chapter 13. But that is rare. Usually the stop order will serve you much better. Almost always it will be better to admit we are never going to catch the extremes, and only want a piece out of the middle of the move.

TYPES OF STOP ORDERS

We are going to look at three different types of stop orders to exit positions. They are all very closely related and very similar, but their placement is a little different in each case. They are:

1. Stop-loss orders
2. Trailing stops
3. Profit-taking stops

First let us look at the stop-loss order. It is typically placed soon after a position is entered, and is designed to protect against a move in the wrong direction and to correct a mistake in entering the position. Many people set their stops at a particular percentage away from the original entry level, saying that they will not accept more than a predetermined percentage risk. The problem with this practice is that all stocks do not have the same level of volatility. In one company a 10 percent move is gigantic, while in another it is commonplace. If an investor will not accept more than a certain amount of risk, it is better to select stocks that are likely to be less risky, rather than to arbitrarily impose that percentage on every stock. Stop levels need to be tailored to each individual situation. When I am considering a possible buy, I first determine where I want to put in my entry stop order. Then, before doing anything else, I determine where my stop-loss order should be, based on the stock, its chart, and its history. If the potential loss is larger than I feel comfortable with, I eliminate the stock as a possible trade.

There are a number of other, much more sophisticated ways of placing stops based on such methods as standard deviations. The use of standard deviations is better than a set percentage because it is matching the stop to the nature of the stock. However, I feel the best approach is one of logic. We know a great deal about the typical price action of a company, based on chart patterns and volume characteristics. I would rather tailor the stop levels using that knowledge than rely on a mathematical formula.

I am bothered every time one of my stop orders to get out is executed. I shouldn't be, because it is part of my plan, but I always do have that feeling. It seems, at the time, as though it is a sign of failure. I have been taken out of a stock because it was going down when I thought it should go higher, or I was taken out of a short position because it was going up when I thought it should go down. That is what makes this discipline difficult to follow. Almost always, within a few minutes, hours, or days, I am congratulating myself on getting out before I was hurt much worse. And even though I am aware that it usually works that way, it is still not easy to watch a position be taken away by a stop order. In the preceding chapter we were talking about stop orders to get into a position, and the fact that it was psychologically difficult to offer to pay up for a stock when it could be bought at a cheaper price by just guessing at the likely up move. But, in that case, it is a new position without the additional psychological burden of ownership. Once I own a stock I have made a commitment, and I want to be right. Even if no one else knows what I am doing, I feel somewhat accountable to myself. For that reason, the most important rule in placing stop orders to get out is to *place them immediately*. The first instant you own a stock is the time when you can be the most objective about it. As soon as you have owned it for a little while and watched a few up or down moves, it becomes more difficult to decide unemotionally where to place the stop. That is another reason I prefer to have already determined my stop-loss level before I even enter the stop order to get in. Then, as soon as I have a confirmed entry, I immediately enter the predetermined stop.

LOGICAL ORDER PLACEMENT

Stop-loss orders should be entered based on the chart. Looking at the picture, I ask myself what would have to happen for me to know that I had been wrong in entering the position. Then I give it a small amount of leeway from there, to allow for extraneous ripples, and set my stop-loss level. Usually the first determination gives me a round number, but knowing that round numbers have an uncanny way of being touched, I usually give the stock a few cents of room away from the round number.

Because we are generally buying a stock because of a power box, the placement of the stop is likely to be obvious.

On the chart of Citigroup in 2006 (Figure 11.1), we have a very common scenario. The horizontal line is the resistance level going back many months. It is decisively penetrated in early December, with a large trading range and heavy volume. There can be little doubt that this is a power box. It pulls back for just two days, but that gives us time to determine the slope of the descending top of the consolidation. So the stock is bought when it moves up through that descending line the next day. This is a great setup, because the stop can be placed below the last level of support, which is just about a point below where we bought. The risk is therefore only about 2 percent. If the stock decides it is not going up, we will be taken out with a small loss, but the stock has already told us it wants to go higher. In this case it did, indeed, move sharply higher, producing a good profit. That is the nice thing about using small flags, rectangles, and pennants after a breakout as an area in which to be buying. In the case of a flag or rectangle the stop is quite close to the

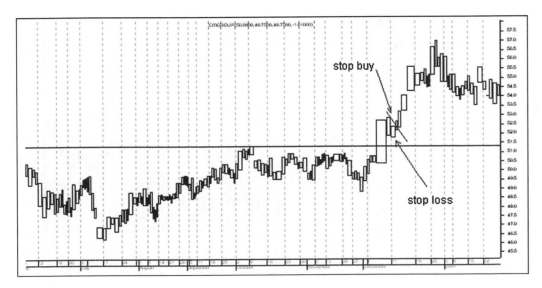

FIGURE 11.1 Breakout through Resistance.

entry point, and in the case of a pennant it is extremely close to the entry point. Yet a change of direction has occurred, so we are in harmony with the rhythm of the stock.

On the chart of CEC Entertainment (Figure 11.2), we have two examples, one a short and the other a long. The first is brought to our attention by a power box to the downside; it becomes a candidate for a short sale. The next two days give us a small flag, but, as is usual with a flag during a decline, it is waving up rather than down. The break below the bottom of the flag triggers a stop sell to get us into the short position. That leads us to immediately place a protective stop just a few cents above the last resistance level, the top of the flag. From here the stock continues lower, never hitting our protective stop and allowing us later to move that stop lower.

Two months later we have a new situation, in which the stock has shown us a power box to the upside. After that strength, the consolidation is a small pennant rather than a flag. We are put into the stock when the upper limits of the pennant are broken. Because the lows have been ascending, we are able to place our stop-loss order very close without going against the conclusions we reached through our analysis.

These are all examples in which the stop order was placed but never used. There are times, though, when the stop serves its purpose of minimizing our losses. We see that in the chart of Champion Enterprises, in Figure 11.3.

Everything seemed to be favorable as this stock broke out with a pair of heavy-volume up days. The pullback was a typical flag that lasted about three weeks. The breakout above the descending top of the flag put us in at a favorable level, and we

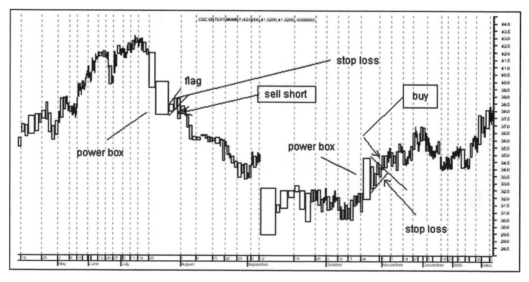

FIGURE 11.2 A Short and a Long.

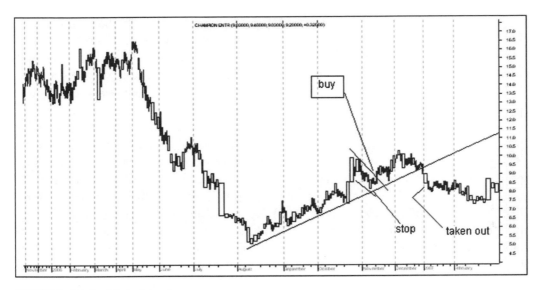

FIGURE 11.3 Minimizing Losses.

would have immediately placed a stop just below the prior low. From there the stock did move higher, but then failed. As we will see next, we might have moved the stop up below each of those small pullback lows, thereby capturing a profit. But, assuming we did not, we would have been stopped out when the stock started to go back down. The result would have been a loss, but a very small loss. The protective stop did its job.

I suggest readers take time to go to their computers and bring up, randomly, a large number of charts, looking for power boxes and identifying the subsequent consolidations, and then establishing logical levels for initial stop orders. It is surprising, doing this exercise, to observe how few of those stops get picked off immediately. In most cases the price continues to move enough to provide a profit and to allow for the protection of that profit by moving the stop. The trick is to move the stop enough to protect the profit, but not so much as to be taken out prematurely.

TRAILING STOPS

Basically, after the original stop is placed, we want to move the stop in the direction that continues to protect more of our money. Each time a minor pullback and resumption of the move is seen, we want to move our stop to a point just beyond where the turn occurred. The assumption is that both an up move and a down move are a series of steps, each progressively producing a little more profit. That means, though, that we cannot act immediately. Only after the stock has had time to make its next pullback do we have the information to know where the next turning point lies. It is never correct to move the stop order down in a long position or up in a short position. That is called rationalization of an unfavorable move. The first placement of the stop was the detached and unemotional one. The idea is to follow the move and be taken out as soon as a lower low in an advancing stock or higher high in a declining stock is seen.

Look, for instance, at the chart of CIT Group (Figure 11.4). Throughout the entire move the stock never made a pullback low until the advance finally came to a decisive conclusion. There was one pullback that made a very similar low, and would have been worrisome, but turned out to be just a resting phase about midway in the advance.

Of course, sometimes it does not work that smoothly. Consider the chart of Geron Corporation in 2006 and 2007 (Figure 11.5). Here we followed the rules. We bought on the top of the flag, after the power box. We placed our stop and then moved it up once when a higher low was made. But then, even though the stock went higher and we had no lower lows, the pullback in early December wiped out all the paper profits from the prior two months. It did not make a new low, so we held on and later moved the stop up once more, finally getting out in January with a small profit after all. Sometimes the system of putting your stop under each pullback low will get you out too soon, but generally it is effective. It is not a bad thing to get out early if you have a profit. The fact you were taken out implies the stock is not acting as expected or hoped. You can move the money to another situation, a new power box, and start the process again.

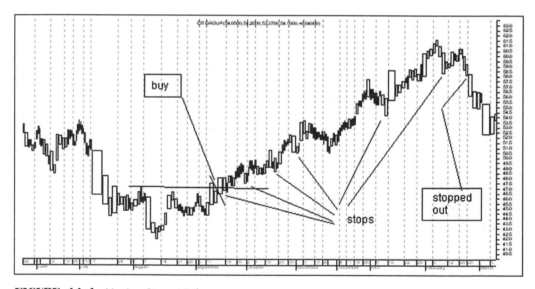

FIGURE 11.4   Moving Stops Higher.

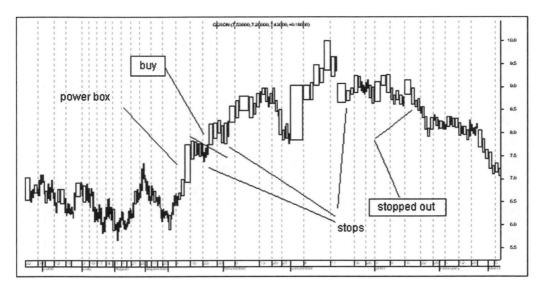

FIGURE 11.5 Geron, 2006–2007.

PROFIT-TAKING STOPS

The problem with a trailing stop such as we have just looked at is that it tends to leave quite a bit of money on the table at the end of the move. The reason for that is that very often the final part of an advance or decline is an accelerated move, leading to a spike. The top or bottom of that spike can represent a large part of the overall move. That is why I also have included the possibility of placing a profit-taking stop. This order should be entered only when it looks as though the move has gone too far too fast. It is not based on the pattern of ascending lows or descending highs; it is based on the desire to maximize profits while still allowing for more progress in case we are wrong. As an example, Figure 11.6 shows Principal Financial's stock in early 2007.

It had been a strong uptrend, so a long position could have been followed nicely with a trailing stop order. Then the stock seemed to shift to high gear and trend upward with a much steeper pattern. It could still be followed with a stop below each pullback to protect the gain. However, then it posted a very square Equivolume entry that penetrated the ascending trend line. That was a strong indication that the stock had encountered heavy overhead resistance. The exiting stop would have still nailed down a good profit, but it looked better, at the time, to give the stock almost no room to move back down, and thereby to maximize profits. A plain sell order would have removed the opportunity to profit if the advance continued, but a close stop would get the stock sold at the least sign of weakness. The latter is what happened.

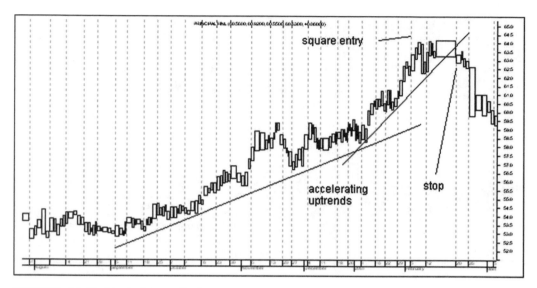

FIGURE 11.6   Maximizing a Profit.

A profit-taking stop can maximize profits, but it carries the danger of getting out too soon in a very strong stock. The technique should be used only in unusual circumstances, and we should guard against using it as an excuse to give in to our natural inclination to nail down a profit. It borders on second-guessing, which we do not want to do.

Remember to never be long or short any stock without having a stop order protecting you. Early in the game it can save you from a big loss. During the move it will protect you from the unexpected unfavorable move that can erase much of your gain. And late in the game it can help you to maximize your profits. Moreover, you can walk away from the markets and go on a vacation and know that you are not likely to be badly hurt.

CHAPTER 12

A Play, Not a Position

One of the hardest lessons I have had to learn over the years has been patience. It is never difficult to find a position to go into, but it is very difficult to stay with that position when it is going with you. Profits are enticing. I had to learn that I should look at the initiation of a position as a possible start to a larger program—a play in that stock, not just a position. The temptation is to buy a full position, watch it move, and take the profit on the position or get stopped out of the position a short time later. Often that approach can be profitable, but the danger is that your gains and losses will be about the same size, and will tend to offset one another. The really big profits come when a long move occurs and you are able to not only stay with it, but parlay your position. Then a position becomes a play. It goes back to one of Wall Street's oldest, but best, adages: Cut your losses short and let your profits run.

SOME BASIC RULES

It is not easy to state a rule for stock market action. Rules do not always hold true. But there are certainly a few tendencies that are so strong we can use them. Here are a few:

- Trends are more likely to continue than they are to reverse.
- Volume tends to be in the direction of movement.
- Many times an advance or a decline is announced by a power box.
- Countertrend moves are to be expected.
- Most moves have a number of spurts, interspersed with consolidations.

As we saw in Chapter 8 on power boxes, a big volume day with a wide trading range and an obvious change of direction or penetration of resistance is a very reliable sign it is time to move into that stock as a buy or a sell, depending on the direction of the box. The power box is telling us that something has changed. It is not the same stock after the power box as it was before. That power box suggests that a new move may be starting that will have longer-term implications. So, if we treat the action after the power box as though it were just a continuation of the same swings we were seeing before it, we may miss the big move—the play.

If you were wildcatting for oil, you would drill a large number of exploratory holes. Many would be dry holes, and a few would be good producers. But once in a while you would hit a big one—a gusher. When that happened, you would not just move on to another prospect; you would drill a number of offset holes in the same area. You would realize you were on an unusual structure, and you would try to make the most of it. Instead of a single well, it would be an oil field. We are looking for the occasional oil fields in the stock market, and want to take advantage of them when they come along.

Like drilling the offset wells, the play consists of a number of entries at various levels. It means that if a long position, for instance, is going with you, you are going to commit a larger percentage of your money to a single position. You want to turn the single well into a profitable oil field. But it also means starting small, and risking more only when you are winning. It allows you to look at each new position as a possible play. It also means that if the play does not work out, you will get out and move along without taking a disastrous loss. Because a power box, by its nature, means a radical change in the stock, there is a good possibility that there is a big reward to be garnered. But jumping in with a big initial position, based on a feeling that it is going to be a huge winner, is very dangerous. Buying a smaller amount, and adding to it if you are proven right, means you will pay higher prices for your later additions, but you will have limited your risk.

EXAMPLES

The chart of Boeing (Figure 12.1) gives us a good example of a play rather than just a buy. On the first day in February of 2006, Boeing suddenly moved higher with very heavy volume. The trading range expanded dramatically, and it even left a gap behind. It was easy to see a change had suddenly occurred and to anticipate that it might lead to a substantial advance. The next day the stock hesitated and then backed off on lighter volume for a couple of days. By placing a stop buy order just above that small downtrend line, we anticipated that the first buy would be made at about $72 when there was the first sign of renewed strength. Using the stop buy ensured that if the stock had just gone back down we never would have bought the stock. So we were buying strength, not weakness. The first buy was only about one-third of the position we would like to have

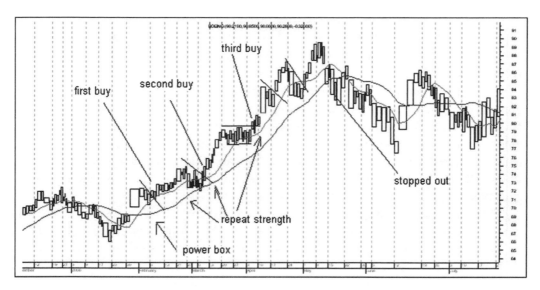

FIGURE 12.1 A Play in Boeing.

if the position was going to work. We could buy more later if the stock acted right, but if it failed we were not going to take too big a hit. Our possible loss was limited by the fact that we had placed a stop-loss sell order just below the last support, at about $70.

The stock did move higher, and showed another impressive burst of strength almost a month later. That again looked like a sign of strength and prompted us to watch for a chance to add to the position. Again we had a lighter-volume pullback—a flag—that allowed us to see a series of descending tops. We placed our second buy order, again a stop buy, just above that line, and we soon owned the second part of our position at about $75 per share. Of course we immediately moved our stop-loss order up to the previous support level, $72.

After another nice rise, the stock entered a lateral consolidation. When it went through the top of that small rectangle it looked as though that would be an opportune time to round out the position. Again with a stop buy order, the last one-third was bought at about $80 and the protective stop was immediately raised to $77.50. This was the last purchase, even though, as it worked out, there were three more up legs to the advance. As it gets later in a play, the risks of a downturn increase. Even though most advances of this sort tend to last about five legs, the later buys can still be unprofitable, because we are relying on a stop to take us out. We know, as a consequence, that we will never sell at the top. Therefore, I like to end the program at the third buy. Then it is just a question of following the action with a trailing stop. As it gets later I often move the stop in a bit closer so as to not leave too much profit on the table. Here we would have moved the stop up each time an intermediate-term higher low was made. The subsequent stops were at $82 and then at $83. That way, anytime a lower low rather than a higher low was made, we would be stopped out. In this case, we saw a lower low at the end of May and were stopped out at $83.

Our average purchase price was $75.66 and our sale was at $83, over a period of four months. If we had bought the entire position in the beginning, at $72, we would have made a good deal more money, but we would have assumed a far larger risk. As it was done, our largest risk was two points on a one-third position. The second position was at a three-point risk when it was put on, but the first part of the position was at a three-point profit by then. The third position was at a 2.5-point risk, but the other two positions were at an average profit of four points each.

There is usually no way of knowing when we are going to hit a gusher rather than a good producer or a dry hole. That is why we need to drill cheap holes first. But the huge producers seem most often to come when a long-dormant stock suddenly becomes interesting. Without ever knowing the fundamentals that cause the power box, we know that something has changed radically. Let's look at such a case.

In September 2006, W. R. Grace was a quiet, uninteresting, prosaic stock that certainly did not look as though it could do much. (See Figure 12.2.) But then it suddenly produced a power box. In two days it went from 11 to 13 with very heavy volume. The second day also took it through the top of a long-lasting consolidation zone. The stock looked like a buy, but it had already moved so far it was hard to just jump in. However,

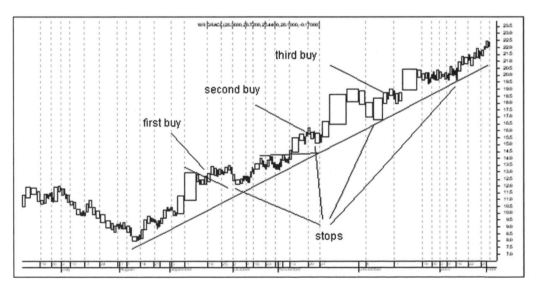

FIGURE 12.2 Three Buys in W. R. Grace.

FIGURE 12.3 A Short Play in Pixelworks.

in the next three days it pulled back a little and volume became much lighter, which was a good sign. The first logical buy would be a stop buy order just above that small decline. That meant a buy at about 13 with a stop at the prior support around 12. Again, as in the prior example, there turned out to be a series of up steps in the stock, allowing two more buys and a trailing stop that did not get hit. There was virtually no way to anticipate that this stock would have a very big move. But the volume and the price move alerted us that something was going on. This was a sleeper that suddenly woke up. What looked as though it would be a small move turned out to be a bonanza play.

The same technique can be used on the short side. Figure 12.3 shows how Pixelworks lost half its value over a five-month period. The stair-step down pattern provided the opportunity to go in repeatedly, following the stock down. But the big plays to the downside are less common.

A WORD OF CAUTION

Not every trade that emerges because of a power box is going to turn into a bigger play. We need to follow a strategy that allows us to use the attractive power boxes with the intention of following along and turning a simple single position into a multiple position only when everything goes right. We must follow our discipline, investing our money in drilling a number of wells simultaneously, knowing that some will be dry holes and some will be producers. When we tap a promising new field, we need to be aware we have done so and commit a larger part of our capital to that play.

There is one additional benefit in looking for the bigger plays. Our outlook tends to change, so that we are in less of a hurry to get out with a small profit. The natural tendency to want to nail down a profit is replaced by, or at least subdued by, the desire to add to a winner.

CHAPTER 13

Minding the Gaps

O ne of the most apparent features on a stock chart is a gap. Consequently, gaps have been in the forefront of the thinking of many stock technicians for as long as the discipline has existed. Little is said about volume in most of the literature, yet volume appears to be the key to the interpretation of gaps. Classic texts on technical analysis, and even recent volumes, go into great detail about the classification and inter- pretation of gaps with hardly a mention of volume. As we will see in this chapter, it is the combination of volume and trading range, along with the components of Equivolume entries, that allows us to see what sort of gap we are dealing with and gain a sense of the likely future action of the stock.

WHAT IS A GAP?

A gap is simply a price range in which no trading occurred. For example, an opening gap is often seen, based on an overnight change in attitude, either toward the markets in general or toward that particular stock. The stock closes at its high on one day and then opens on the next day at a higher price (or it closes at its low and then opens at a lower price), leaving a range of prices in which there was no trading. It appears on the chart as just that, a gap in the flow of prices. Once you are aware of gaps, they will seemingly demand your attention.

Let's look at the traditional classification of gaps (see Figure 13.1):

- *Trading range gaps.* These gaps are usually seen within a sideways consolidation. They are very common, are usually small, and do not represent any dramatic change

FIGURE 13.1 Gaps on a Bar Chart.

in the stock. They can be caused by a stock going ex-dividend, or they can occur because the stock is inactive or because it is a stock that trades on other markets when our markets are closed. Trading range gaps are more common in some stocks than in others, and can usually be considered meaningless.

- *Breakaway gaps.* These gaps are usually seen at the beginning of an advance or a decline. They occur when a stock breaks out of a consolidation, and they represent a change in the trading habits of the stock. An important support or resistance level is usually broken in the process. Breakaway gaps are quite common and are very important. They come in early in a move that is often long and strong.

- *Runaway gaps.* These are usually seen later in a move, and are less common. They occur when a stock has so much strength or weakness that it is metaphorically running away. Runaway gaps are sometimes called measuring gaps, because they often come in just about midway in a decline or an advance. Therefore, if a gap can be identified as a runaway gap, it is a clue that the move is about half over and that there is still room to make money.

- *Exhaustion gaps.* These gaps come late in a decline or an advance. They represent the last surge of strength in the case of an advance, or weakness in a decline, prior to a turnaround. The problem is that they look a great deal like a runaway gap, so they are often identified only in retrospect. Retrospect doesn't help to make successful trades.

We will use these classifications, with some modifications based on volume and trading range.

IDENTIFYING GAPS

What is really needed is a method of better identifying each gap. Let's look at some gaps, but on an Equivolume basis.

Figure 13.2 shows a number of trading range gaps. Notice that we have two boxes enclosing each gap that are, in themselves, quite ordinary. Neither trading range nor volume is expanding greatly; the boxes on the two sides of each gap are similar in size and shape. Now, through volume and price, we have been able to classify the gaps, and have ruled them out as having any strong message for our consideration.

The first gap on this chart looks like an exhaustion gap. It is the final downward move before support is found. But what would make us recognize it as an exhaustion gap rather than a runaway gap? The answer is the combination of box sizes and shapes on the two sides of the gap. The stock gaps lower, but finds a very heavy buying interest just below. That causes an Equivolume entry that is short and wide. Short and wide boxes are seen when there is an intense standoff between buyers and sellers. Price movement has become difficult. Usually the day before that standoff is a day of easy movement, so our next rule is that an exhaustion gap is typified by a tall and relatively narrow box preceding the gap, and then a short and fat box after the gap. In addition, it is noticeable that the gaps that turn out to be exhaustion gaps are generally very large.

The last of the gaps labeled as a trading range gap seems to meet the requirements of an exhaustion gap based on box sizes and shapes. In fact, it does represent a temporary

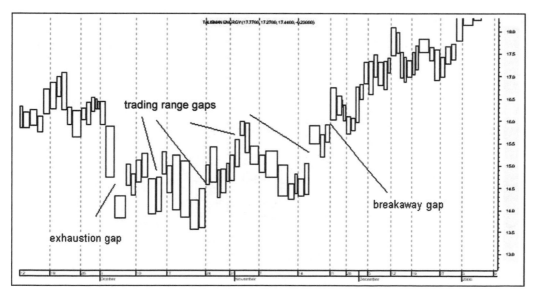

FIGURE 13.2 Trading Range Gaps, Exhaustion Gap, and Breakaway Gap.

stopping point. But it is different in that it is not the culmination of powerful move, and no important levels are penetrated. It is perhaps a precursor of the breakaway gap that comes in just three days later, but it is not a signal to do anything.

The last gap in Figure 13.2 is a breakaway gap. The distinguishing characteristics of a breakaway gap are a smaller box, usually short and narrow, before the gap, followed by a taller and wider box after the gap. It represents a change, in that volume and trading range have both become larger as a new buying interest enters the stock. Of course, the breakaway gap is usually pointing us to a power box after the gap, another of our indicators.

Finally, we have the runaway gaps shown in Figure 13.3. On the right side of the gap we usually see a box, or a series of boxes, that are quite tall and wide, indicating increasing strength. Then, after the gap, we see a powerful continuation of the strength. Sometimes the box size will increase across the gap, making it look more like a break-away gap, but it is not breaking away from anything. The more important comparison is to an exhaustion gap, since the distinction could be expensive. The box after the runaway gap is tall, while the box after the exhaustion gap is short and fat. Notice on this chart the way in which the runaway gaps have come in just about halfway through each move.

It is the exhaustion gap that has been most responsible for the erroneous belief that gaps always have to be filled. (See Figure 13.4.) Very often a gap is never filled, or filled so much later as to be of no importance to the trader. Often a breakaway gap is filled in the ensuing pullback, which, of course, plays to our advantage; but there is absolutely no

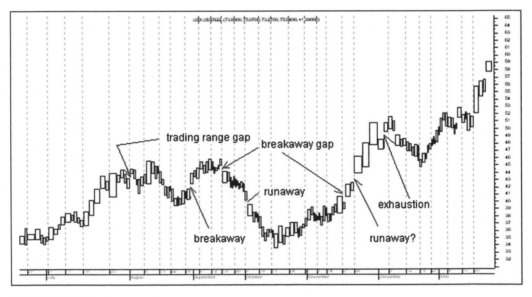

FIGURE 13.3 Runaway Gaps.

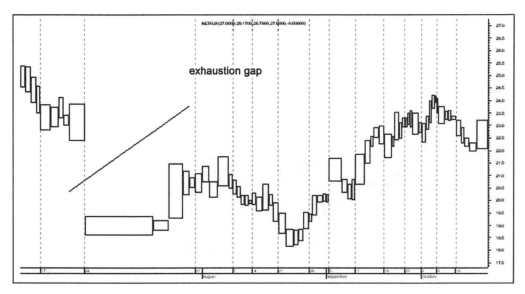

FIGURE 13.4 Exhaustion Gap.

requirement that the area of no trading be traversed again. Runaway gaps, by contrast, usually are not filled until much later, when the stock has entered an entirely new trading phase.

For example, a runaway gap to the upside may be filled much later after the stock has made a top and is in the throes of a declining phase. Trading range gaps are filled in the normal course of trading because they were meaningless in the first place. The important filling of a gap is the trading after an exhaustion gap, because it is part of a reversal in direction, which is what the exhaustion gap was telling us anyway. So the filling of the gap just confirms what we already suspected.

EXPANDING OUR ORIGINAL DEFINITIONS

As an addendum to the earlier list of gap types and their recognition, we need to add the Equivolume characteristics (Figure 13.5):

- *Trading range gaps.* Small box to small box across the gap.
- *Breakaway gaps.* Small box to big powerful box across the gap.
- *Runaway gaps.* Powerful box to another powerful box across the gap.
- *Exhaustion gaps.* Tall box to short wide box across the gap.

Gaps can be extremely useful. Very successful traders have told me that they use the aforementioned method of classification and then base a great deal of their trading on

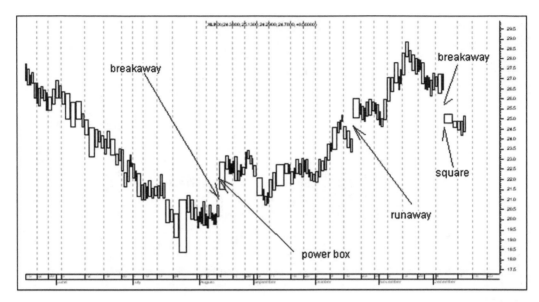

FIGURE 13.5 Gaps during an Advance.

which kind of gap they are observing. Of course, if they are looking for a breakaway gap as the buy signal they are also inadvertently looking for power boxes. But by looking only for the gaps they may be missing some great power box breakouts that do not start with a gap. I suggest using the gaps as very helpful and accurate signals, but basing decisions on more factors than the gaps alone.

In trading, gaps become a very valuable tool, but usually a confirming tool, not an action-originating tool. We need to always be aware when a gap occurs. The first step then is to classify the gap. Using the aforementioned guidelines, it is usually quite easy to place the gap in one category or another:

- We can usually ignore trading range gaps.
- A breakaway gap is, of course, the one we are going to be most excited about, because it is so often associated with a power box. It is another sign of the strength that has generated the move.
- The runaway gap is telling us that we have a very strong position. It usually comes after we have a substantial profit on paper, and has the addition benefit that it gives us a measuring point. In that a runaway gap tends to come midway in a move, it tells us a possible target.
- The exhaustion gap is a warning. It suggests it might be a good time to tighten up our stop order from a trailing stop to a profit-taking stop.

CHAPTER 14

Tops and Bottoms

How do we know a stock has made a top? The answer is: "When it is going down." Conversely, we know a stock has made a bottom when it has started to go up. This is not a very satisfactory answer; it is one that can be improved upon. But the problem is real. A consolidation is just that, a sideways trading range that either interrupts or reverses a trend. The difficulty is in determining whether it is doing the former or the latter; however, there are clues that can help.

IDENTIFYING TOPS AND BOTTOMS

We do know that there are about twice as many consolidations followed by a resumption of the move as there are times the consolidation is followed by a reversal of direction. This fact dictates, therefore, that we should be biased in the direction of a continuation, and not be too quick to think that the move is over and it is time to take the profits. That is one of the main reasons we are usually so much better off if we use stops instead of making predictions. Using stops helps us to go with the move and recognize that the trend really is our friend most of the time. Sometimes, though, the way in which prices move and the way in which volume comes in give us valuable information about the probable direction.

Because we are talking about a particular technique for trading, it narrows the concern somewhat. If we are not long or short a particular stock, it does not much matter whether we are looking at a resting phase or a reversal; and we are not going to be in a stock unless we have had a strong reason to be. So it is only after we have gone into a stock that we want to know if a consolidation means that our stock is going to continue to move along or turn in the other direction. We do not have to be concerned with the consolidations of a stock that is oscillating indecisively in a trading range if we have already eliminated that stock as a candidate.

In addition, we have agreed that we will always have a stop order in, and we will get out of a position only with the use of a stop. Therefore, is it really important to classify each consolidation? Not if we are willing to settle for a modest profit. But there are times when it means leaving a great deal of the profit on the table. If we can observe the nature of a consolidation, it may help, especially late in a move, to maximize our profits.

If we are buying a stock, it is generally because we are seeing a heavy-volume move to the upside. From there, if it is doing as expected, volume is likely to be heavier on the upswings than on the downswings. We see that in Figure 14.1, a chart of Humana in 2005 and 2006.

Each of the consolidations gave us another stair step in a series of higher lows, and allowed a trailing stop order that did not take us out. But the consolidation in early February was attention getting. Volume suddenly became very heavy to the downside, which was something unseen for the prior three months as the stock advanced. No lower low had been made yet, so no stop was activated. This would seem to be reason enough, though, to move a stop right under the low of that day. Two days later the position was sold on the stop.

Another clue that the advance in Humana was ending was the penetration of the ascending trend line. Often stocks will give us very reliable patterns like this, so that a

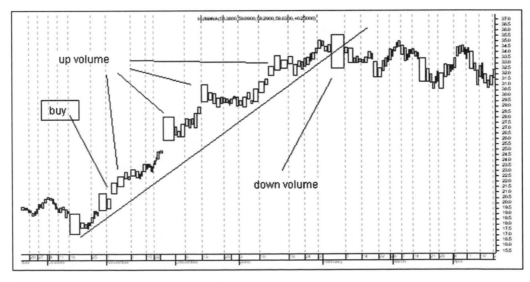

FIGURE 14.1 A Change in Volume Direction.

change of direction becomes very apparent. Interestingly, the stock moved sideways for about three months and then resumed the advance, as shown in Figure 14.2.

Does that mean it was wrong to sell it? I do not think so. A period of three months in which no money was being made was avoided. It would have been possible, and technically justifiable, to come back in on the next sign of strength and ride the subsequent advance.

On the chart of Starwood Hotels in 2002 (Figure 14.3), we see the way in which, at just about the center of the chart, there was a shift from upside volume to downside volume. It made it look as though the advance was coming to a close and a decline was about to begin. This chart also serves to illustrate another point. The top made at that time has the look of a head and shoulders—that is, three highs, with the middle one higher than the other two. Notice the decreasing volume across the three highs and the establishment of a flat pair of lows that could be construed as a neckline. The head and shoulders is just one of many types of double and triple tops that can form, but it has a particularly strong success record. That gives extra validity to the move to the downside out of the consolidation, and suggests going short.

The final low of the decline was on extremely heavy volume, which suggested the sellers were dumping stock indiscriminately and hinted at a possible reversal. Two days later the advance was not spectacular, but broke the steepest descending trend line and implied a reversal might have started. It would be enough evidence to warrant moving a buy stop order in quite close if we were short.

In Figure 14.4, a chart of DuPont, a reverse head and shoulders gave us a good clue that a significant bottom was being made. The power box up with the breakaway gap took the stock decisively through the neckline and prompted a buy.

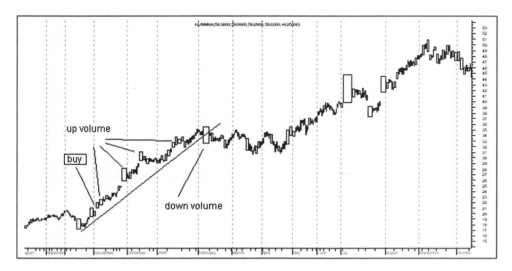

FIGURE 14.2 Breaking the Trend Line.

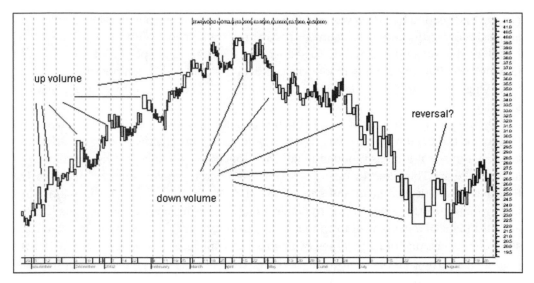

FIGURE 14.3 Up Volume Becomes Down Volume.

FIGURE 14.4 A Head and Shoulders Bottom.

The high after this advance showed, though, that all reversals are not so easy to spot. The only indications that it was over were the breaking of the ascending trend line and the increase in volume to the downside. Luckily, we had placed a stop under that pullback low, so the second down move triggered that stop and preserved most of the profit.

The tops and bottoms we have been looking at here are generally larger formations. They are often hard to decipher. In addition, every up or down move is punctuated by much smaller consolidations that are so likely to be just pauses without a change of direction that they are often referred to as continuation patterns. Of course, they too can be reversals, but more often they are not. These shorter-term consolidations are the subject of the next chapter.

CHAPTER 15

Flags, Pennants, and Rectangles

Technicians usually classify consolidations in two ways. The first is based on the length of time involved, and the second is based on the structure of the consolidation. The longer-term consolidations are usually put into categories, such as wedges, triangles, or large rectangles. The shorter-term consolidations are usually looked at as flags, pennants, or rectangles. It is interesting that most traditional technicians pay very little attention to volume, especially as it relates to consolidations. They do pay closer attention to volume when a stock is moving up or down, since volume appears to give an indication of power or lack of power. But that same power, or lack of power, is evident in consolidations, and is often a clue as to whether the eventual breakout and move is more likely to be to the upside or to the downside. We know, of course, that any consolidation is twice as likely to be followed by a continuation of direction than by a reversal. So it is safer to assume a continuation. But at times the volume action belies that assumption. It becomes an alert as to probable direction.

MINOR CONSOLIDATIONS

Let us first go to the smallest formations. These are the minor consolidations, lasting a few days to a few weeks, with an average size of around three weeks. If a stock is moving higher after a breakout, for example, it will often pause along the way. Interestingly, these pauses are usually not sideways moves; more often they are countertrend moves. Typically they take the form of flags, pennants, or sometimes small rectangles.

How do we spot the start of a small sideways formation as it develops? The answer is volume. It is a formation that follows an entry with heavier than usual volume and a larger than usual price move. That gives us a sort of flagpole (on the downside it is an upside-down flagpole). It is a burst of energy that is often followed by a period of consolidation. That consolidation takes the shape of a flag, a pennant, or a rectangle, suspended from the end of the flagpole.

THE TYPICAL FLAG

After we have bought a stock, we need to be on the lookout for pauses, and we must attempt to categorize them. The clue that tells us a consolidation is developing is a heavy-volume day with a big price range that is tall enough to look like a flagpole. From there it is likely a flag or a pennant will eventually dangle. It is as though a great deal of energy is suddenly expended, and then the traders sit back and rest for a while. Therefore, the consolidation is expected to be on lighter volume. The very fact that we have unusually heavy volume followed by lighter trading is a message that we are apparently entering a resting phase; the aggressive buyers have backed away. So, as soon as we see heavy volume, we should be looking to see what the next action is. If it is, as we so often see, lighter trading, then we should start to watch carefully and try to classify the character of the subsequent action. It will most likely be a flag—that is, a move in which the highs and lows of a number of days or weeks are parallel, but counter to the overall trend.

On a rising stock, the series of entries looks like a flag hanging down from the flagpole, which was the heavy-volume day that got our attention in the first place. The flag is very normal behavior, and usually is a sign the move is going to continue. As we will see, the light-volume pullback is usually a continuation pattern, not a reversal pattern. So we want to see that slowing of volume. In fact, if the volume is too heavy in the consolidation, it is a warning that things are not right. Heavier volume rather than lighter volume is telling us that the pullback is attracting too much trading, so it may be the beginning of a reversal rather than just a normal consolidation.

DIFFERENT TYPES OF CONSOLIDATIONS

In Figure 15.1, we see a number of different types of consolidations occurring in DuPont stock in late 2005 and early 2006.

Let us look first at the flags. They are the most common type of short-term consolidation. They are a fair-weather signal hoisted to the top of the flagpole. When we see a typical flag, with the volume properly decreasing, it is suggesting clear sailing ahead. The breakout is very likely to be a continuation, not a reversal. A flag, by definition, consists of parallel lines forming a downward-sloping consolidation in bullish longer-term moves or an upward-sloping consolidation in bearish longer-term moves.

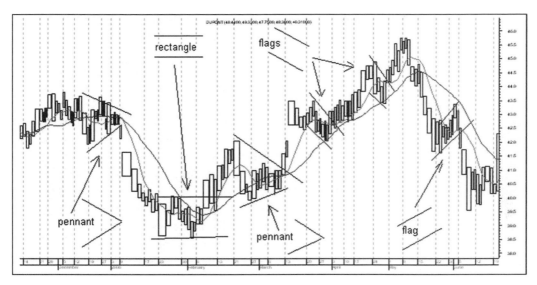

FIGURE 15.1 Consolidations.

MEASURING THE MOVES

An additional aid given by a flag is its ability to indicate the extent of the next advance or decline. This measuring attribute allows us to forecast how far the next leg is likely to go. The leg that leads to the flag is usually about the same size as the leg that follows the flag.

Look at the flags on the DuPont chart (Figure 15.1) and notice how well these measurements worked out. Not only the two flags on the advance, but also the upside-down flag during the decline, occurred just about midway in their respective moves. I suggest going to almost any daily chart and trying to identify flags.

It is helpful to draw in the limits of the tops and bottoms of every minor consolidation, as was done on the DuPont chart. You will see just how numerous flags are and just how well they signal probable moves. Do not ever be reluctant to draw a large number of lines on your charts. A single computer keystroke can get rid of them if you wish, but in the meantime they are helping you to see what is going on. Try to enclose every minor consolidation in a pair of lines.

WRONG-WAY FLAGS

As we noted, though, if a flag does not act right, look out! The danger signs are a flag that does not have decreasing volume, a flag that lasts too long, or a flag that slopes in the wrong direction for the trend in which it is seen. An up flag in an advancing market or a down flag in a declining market might seem to be encouraging, but in reality they are a signal that a change of direction may be starting.

Figure 15.2 (Goldman Sachs in 2005 and 2006) shows a long and strong advance that was punctuated over and over by minor pullbacks. One took the form of a pennant, but all the rest were flags. Each lasted about three weeks, as would be expected, and all except two gave us the typical slowing of volume. The first nonconformist was the second flag from the left. It was bothersome because volume did increase at the end of the formation. It was giving a warning that it might be starting to turn down. However, the advance resumed, and volume improved on the upside. The second nonconformist entry is shown with a question mark. Here volume again increased on the downside. Then the next rally failed at a lower low, and was followed by a break of the bottom of the flag. It was saying that the advance had run into problems, and it was time to take the profit and move on. The flag that had too much volume late in its formation was the clue that something was amiss. We would probably not have acted on it, but it would have sent up a warning: a flag waving a red flag, so to speak.

What about the flag that goes with the trend instead of against the trend? If we see an uptrending flag rather than a pullback flag during a longer-term advance, is it an even more bullish sign? One would think so, since it reflects increased upward pressure. Actually, that is rarely the case. A flag of that sort is actually a warning that all is not as

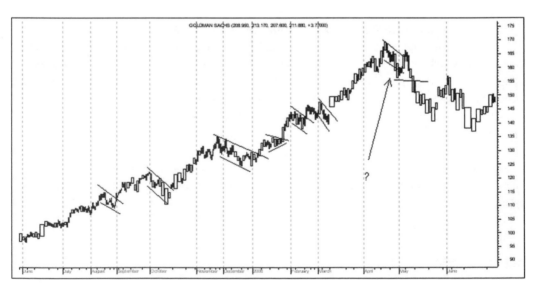

FIGURE 15.2 Pullbacks during a Long Advance.

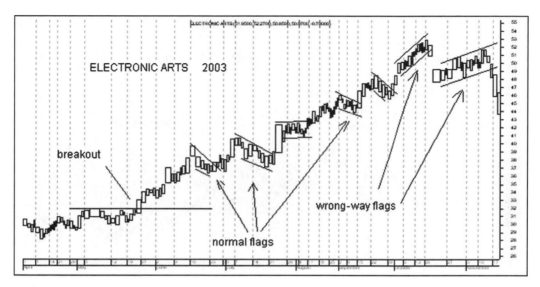

FIGURE 15.3 The End of an Advance.

expected. What we are seeing is a flag that is usually associated with a declining trend, but it is coming in during an advancing trend.

On the chart of Electronic Arts (Figure 15.3), we see a nice breakout from a consolidation, leading to a strong advance. That move was interrupted from time to time by consolidations. All the way up the flags were normal; that is, they sloped away from the dominant direction of the stock. But then after a long advance there were two consolidations that did not look right. They looked more like the flags we would see in the midst of a decline, but they were late in a long advance. The second one was enough of a warning to tell us to get out. There were, of course, other clues to the fact that the advance was ending. One was the gap down on heavy trading, and the other was the lower high on the second wrong-way flag.

FLAGS DURING DECLINES

When we have a stock in a decline rather than an advance, the same observations apply, but in reverse. Take a look at Figure 15.4, which shows Amazon in 2000 and 2001. The stock was just coming off the major top that affected most stocks at that time. All the way down we see a series of countertrend rallies, each telling us the stock is likely to go lower. But then there is a small consolidation that is not the same. It slopes down with the trend, instead of up against the trend. It is saying something is changing. Then the

FIGURE 15.4 The End of a Decline.

consolidations become very small and merge together into a formation that seems to be a rectangle. It takes the price sideways enough to penetrate the descending trend line, and suggests the decline is probably ending. Of course, by then the stock is trading at about one-tenth of its former glory.

As we can see, flags are a very helpful tool. During advances or declines they are very common along the way as confirmations the move is still continuing. Moreover, when a flag is in the wrong direction, if it lasts too long, or if it does not have declining volume, it is very often a sign a move is coming to an end. In monitoring our positions, it is important to keep an eye on the small consolidations, looking for signs of trouble.

PENNANTS AND RECTANGLES

Less common than flags, but still seen very often, are pennants and rectangles. As with the flags, these are short-term consolidations, lasting a few days or a few weeks.

On the chart of Abercrombie & Fitch (Figure 15.5), we are observing a number of pennants and one rectangle. In these formations, we expect to see volume become lower as the move progresses. The odds favor that they are just resting phases within a trend, but that is because the odds of a move out of any consolidation are two to one for a continuation rather than a reversal. So the predictive value of a pennant or rectangle seems to be no better than just the market odds of a continuation rather than a reversal. The problem is that there is no direction to the move itself, so there is no information

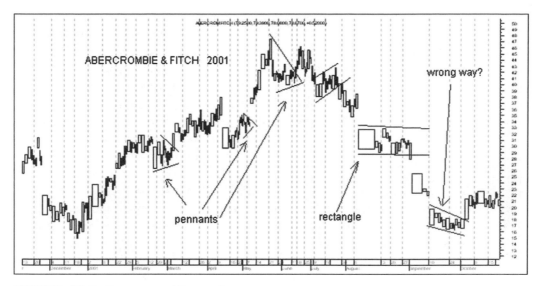

FIGURE 15.5 Pennants and Rectangles.

coming from it. A pennant does not slope either up or down and neither does a rectangle, so there is no additional information imparted.

However, once a trend is established out of a pennant or a rectangle, we still have the measuring effect. As with the flag, if it is a continuation it is likely to put in a second leg of about the same length as the leg that preceded the rectangle or pennant. On the Abercrombie & Fitch chart, we see both as examples. The pennants on the way up were about midway in their respective advances. The rectangle on the way down was just about midway in the total decline.

CONSOLIDATIONS AS A TRADING TOOL

For the very nimble short-term trader, the flags can present an extremely worthwhile opportunity. One can buy while in the flag, assuming the next move will be a continuation move. The odds favor that. Because the flag is usually quite easy to delineate, it is relatively clear when the limits are violated. That in turn makes it possible to recognize trouble quickly and get out with a minimal loss. Because of the ability to project the likely extent of the continuation, when and if it starts, a target can be ascertained. This is a very short-term and aggressive strategy that calls for staying very close to the markets. Also, it means settling for many small profits and losses, and doing a large number of trades. The Equivolume charts are particularly helpful, because the way in which volume is coming in is so important in evaluating a short-term consolidation. It is particularly effective in trading these small formations to use the system of stop order entry, described in Chapter 10. Since the flag is countertrending, you can follow the top of the flag formation down with a stop buy order just above the top of the flag. That means as the flag progresses, you are offering to buy the stock at progressively lower and more advantageous levels. Then, as soon as the trend reverses, you are in. It also gives you a quick idea of the bottom of the pullback, so that you can place your stop-loss order just below it. That way the losses are likely to be small, and the profits are likely to be maximized. If you choose to trade using this method, be sure you look for flags that are forming soon after a change of direction, in order to not be coming in too late in a move.

Boeing (Figure 15.6) could have been a worthwhile trade using this methodology. There was an obvious sign of strength with a heavy-volume upward move that left a breakaway gap behind. A month later the stock started to move sideways and downward in a consolidation. Volume tended to slow as the pullback progressed, and the structure had the downward slope of a typical flag. The odds suggested the stock would resume its upward direction when it completed the consolidation, but there was no way of knowing when that would be. The strategy, then, was to put a buy stop order in just above the line defining the top of the flag. Each day the order could be lowered if a lower high was made. Eventually the breakout did occur and the buy was executed, probably at a better price than if the stock had just been bought at the market price when the possible trade was spotted. Moreover, the stock would not have been bought unless a swing to the

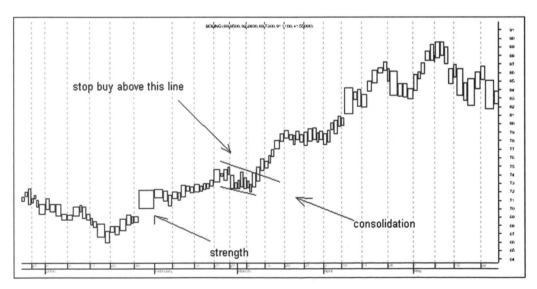

FIGURE 15.6 Buying above the Flag.

upside was strong enough to reverse the downtrend of the flag. If the stock had just slid lower and never reversed, it would never have been bought. Once it broke out from the flag, it looked as though a worthwhile move was under way. From there a close trailing stop could have protected the profit.

The same technique can be used if a pennant formation is seen to be developing. Since the highs are apparently sloping lower, a stop buy order can be placed above the line and can be used to track the slide downward. Any strength through that line triggers a buy. Even though a pennant is not as definitive a continuation sign, it is still right twice as often as it is wrong, so the odds are good. Moreover, since the bottom of the pennant is sloping upward rather than downward, the stop-loss order that is placed after entering the position is likely to be placed at a higher level, thereby making the potential loss smaller.

Even the small rectangular consolidations can be profitable. A stop buy order can be placed just beyond the tops (in the case of a rising stock) so that if the stock appears to be resuming its advance it will be immediately bought. But rectangles tend to be a bit wider, so the stop-loss order will have to be placed a bit further away, somewhat adding to the risk of the trade.

The overall conclusion we reach is that small consolidations tend to be excellent times to plan a strategy. Breakouts from the consolidations tend to be in the direction of the move that led up to them, and they tend to carry far enough to produce a good profit. There is no need to own the stock during the consolidation, since consolidations are times of idle money. But being willing to enter a position as soon as the stock tells us that the consolidation has ended can be very profitable.

The tricky part of trading the moves out of consolidations is getting out of the trade and keeping the profits. Unlike our longer-term trading, covered in other chapters, there are often no reliable signals to tell us a profitable move has ended. There are two things to pay attention to, though. The first is that the leg we are trading is likely to have about the same magnitude as the leg that led up to it. The second is that the duration of the move in terms of volume is likely to be about the same as the volume spent in the consolidation leading up to the move.

CAUSE AND EFFECT

In Figure 15.7, we see how those measurements work out. In this Weight Watchers chart, there appears to be a cause-and-effect relationship in which a certain amount of volume in a consolidation leads to a similar amount of volume in the ensuing advance. We see that the rectangular consolidation shown as period A is just about the same width as the subsequent run-up period marked B. Since width on an Equivolume chart is volume, we are seeing just about the same amount of volume in the consolidation as we are seeing

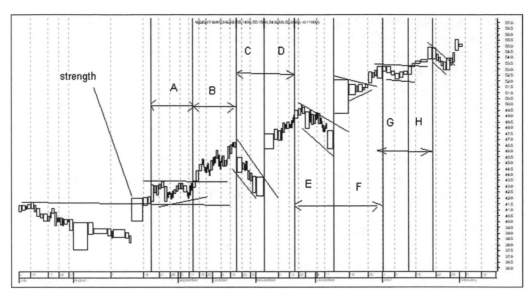

FIGURE 15.7   The Volume-to-Volume Relationship.

in the subsequent advance, regardless of how much time it takes. Similarly, the rest of the consolidations appear to follow the same tendency.

When we look at the vertical dimension, we see that the up moves tend to be similar in extent on the two sides of each consolidation. So, with these two references, we can usually get a good idea of how far a move is likely to go, and how long, in terms of volume, it is going to take. That means we can usually approximate when we want to bail out. And remember, this is a short-term trade. Do not try to turn it into an investment. It is hard to resist the temptation to ride out the next consolidation and see if the stock will then go further. But that should be the subject of another trade, if the conditions justify it. This kind of trading is like winning a ball game with many singles, not with home runs. Trying to stretch a single to a double can mean being thrown out.

There is a time, though, when a consolidation can be traded this way, but in the context of a longer-term position. Consider again the chart of Weight Watchers. Now, though, we are not going to be using the stock as an aggressive short-term trading vehicle. Notice the big box to the far left labeled "strength." The stock was coming off a base and had formed a much larger consolidation, which suggested a lasting advance could be in the cards. Therefore, our desire would be to buy the stock for the longer term. But after the first power box, a consolidation of some sort is usually to be expected. So, when the rectangle in period A starts to develop, we decide to put in a stop buy order just above the top of the consolidation. It is the same strategy as the short-term trading technique we used earlier, but now it is designed to get us in when, and if, the advance continues.

The result is the same—we buy the stock just as it starts to move; but now, instead, we are going to hold it through a number of minor consolidations, if they should occur.

The small consolidations are extremely useful. They are so frequently just resting phases in a move that they are often called continuation patterns. Be sure you identify the nature of each minor consolidation in any stock you own, are short, or are contemplating for a buy or sell. Draw in those many little lines; they will help you to know what is going on.

CHAPTER 16

Support and Resistance

Stocks and stock markets appear to have a memory. It is often uncanny how a particular price level seems to reappear as being important, even many months later. This is so prevalent that we label those levels as support or resistance, depending on whether prices are being held up or held down. In fact, very often, old support levels become new resistance levels and vice versa. Identifying those levels can occasionally be extremely helpful in both going into and going out of a stock. If we can recognize the likely support and resistance levels for the market, it can be an immense aid in our decision making. We see, for example, a series of typical points of support and resistance over a two-year period in Figure 16.1.

Each time the $62 area was approached, it looked as though the stock was encountering a floor. From May to August 2005, it could not drop significantly below that level. Then in September the support level was finally decisively penetrated, which apparently signified a radical change in the stock. For the next year it remained in an entirely different trading range, with the $62 level becoming a barrier to the upside rather than the downside. When it broke out again, this time to the upside, it again seemed to shift to another frame of reference. Recognizing that level, $62, as being important made the breakout very meaningful. Something had happened to change the nature of the stock.

Figure 16.2 gives us a close-up of that breakout. As we can see, the move through the resistance also was done with an increase in volume and a widening trading range, giving it the characteristics of a power box. Recognizing the fact that a level with a great amount of history had been penetrated was an additional piece of information, lending

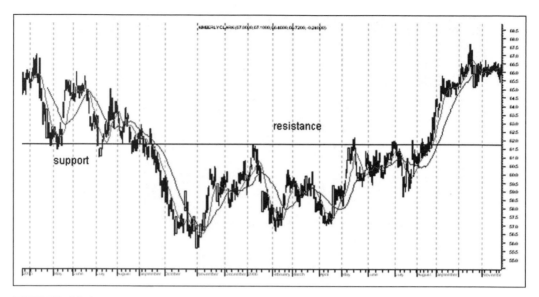

FIGURE 16.1   Support Becomes Resistance.

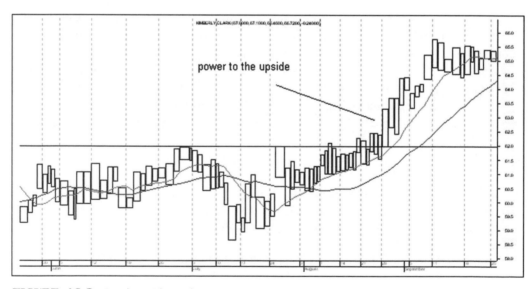

FIGURE 16.2   Breaking Through Resistance.

credence to the idea of a substantial advance being in the offing. The subsequent climb topped out at over $70.

The question, then, is why does the market seem to have a memory for certain levels? It is because the market is reflecting the thoughts of the public, and they have memories. When a level turns a stock down, there is generally a great deal of volume at that point, and all the people who bought at that time are focused on the level as breakeven. A certain number who felt they made a bad investment are going to be saying, "If it ever gets me even, I'm getting out." So it is going to take an inordinate amount of effort to move the stock through the critical level. That is why we look for a volume move through a critical level. I remember in high school physics classes that we learned about "the heat of fusion" of water. It was easy to move the temperature of a quantity of water down the temperature scale until it encountered 32 degrees Fahrenheit and became ice. But the change in temperature to bring about the transition from solid to liquid took about 80 times as much energy. The price point at which a stock moves from solid to liquid, from sleeper to flier, is equally hard to overcome. That is why we look for the spike in energy that alerts us to that transition.

Sometimes we have the solid resistance high opposed by a rising series of low points, as in Figure 16.3. The stock was repeatedly turned back each time it got to the $76 area, but the low became progressively higher, indicating a building of strength. But it still took a great deal of extra energy, energy being represented by volume, to move it out of the trading range and start the rise that followed.

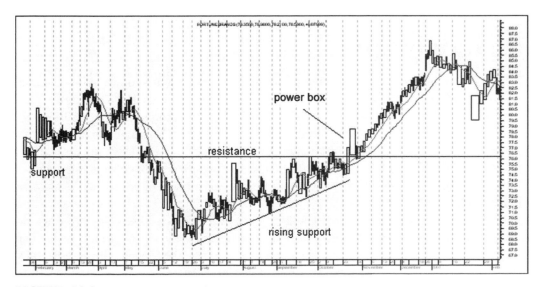

FIGURE 16.3 Energy on the Breakout.

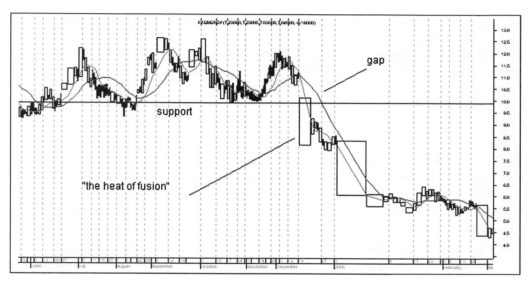

FIGURE 16.4 Breaking Support.

Support, on the way down, works the same way. A stock establishes a level that appears to be important. Many people focus on it, thinking that it is as low as it can go. It takes a great deal of extra energy to melt the ice so that the stock goes tumbling through. We see such a break through the ice in the chart of FX Energy (Figure 16.4).

SHORTER-TERM LEVELS

We have been looking at large and long-lasting moves and major support and resistance levels, but the market memory for price levels is evident at all scales. The ones we are most interested in are the ones that lead to important breakouts. But, in addition, we want to use them as the basis for discerning whether a stock is still acting in our favor. As we saw in the discussion of protective stop orders in Chapter 11, we do not want to stay in a stock if we are long and it makes a lower low, or if we are short and it makes a higher high. In other words, we do not want it to break support or resistance levels on a smaller scale.

For example, if we were short Gannett stock in 2005 (see Figure 16.5), we would have been watching each of those rises that were turned back, establishing a resistance level. As the stock moved lower we would be following with a stop just above those rally tops. Finally, though, a resistance level would not hold. That is when we would want to be out of the short position.

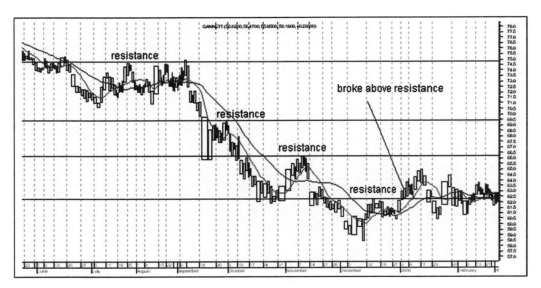

FIGURE 16.5 Shorter-Term Levels.

Support and resistance levels, major and minor, are always with us. They are apparent in every time frame, whether you are looking at weekly charts or at five-minute charts. They represent unchanging levels where buyers and sellers reappear. When those levels are not horizontal but sloped up or down, they become trend lines and channels, which we talk about next.

CHAPTER 17

Trends and Channels

In the prior chapter we were talking about support and resistance levels. They are of great concern to us because they represent the areas that set the stage for the phase we are really interested in. We do not want to buy a stock when it is in a sideways move for two reasons. The first is that if the stock remains sideways for a long time, our money is idle for a long time. We want to be in stocks that are moving, not stocks that are idle. But it is the sideways areas that set up the moves.

Essentially a stock is always doing one of three things. Either it is going up, it is going down, or it is going nowhere. But these three possible conditions are not random. They tend to follow one another and persist for some time once they start. Were it not for the fact that there is a tendency for trends to persist, there would be no way to logically make money trading. What we are really intent upon doing is identifying that trend, agreeing with it and going along with it as long as it lasts, and then when it seems to be changing to another trend, get out of the way. But of the three possible directions, the one we do not want to participate in is the sideways phase. Even in a boring sideways market there are groups and individual stocks that are in an uptrend or a downtrend.

The second reason for not wanting to enter a position while a stock is in a sideways area, stuck between support and resistance levels, is that if we do so, we are trying to guess which way it is going to move when it does move out of the consolidation. As we have discussed, the way in which the volume is coming in can usually give us a good clue as to whether the subsequent move will be up or down, but we are better off, nevertheless, to let the stock itself confirm that for us. Sure, we may be paying up by waiting for the breakout, but we are paying up for a stock that is telling us it wants to move in our direction. When the breakout does occur, we then know not only that the sideways move is over so our money is not likely to lie idle, but we know also which way the stock wants to move.

But the areas we do not want to participate in, the sideways moves, are the areas that give us information about what we want to do. In Chapter 18, when we talk about establishing targets, we will see that the distance a stock moves when it is in a trend is closely related to the size of the consolidation that preceded the trend. So we need to keep an eye on those consolidations.

IDENTIFYING TRENDS

Earlier we identified sideways moves, bases, and tops by the horizontal lines that tended to enclose them. Similarly, advances and declines can be identified by the lines that enclose them: the trend lines and channels. They are very like the lines in the prior chapter except that they slant up or down. It is in these trends that we make our profits.

As we have seen in other parts of our analysis, there are structures within structures in all our charts. This is the fractal nature referred to in Chapter 7. The phenomenon is extremely apparent in looking at trends. For example, in the chart of Google (Figure 17.1), we see that there were two broad consolidation periods, delineated by the horizontal lines, each lasting about three months. But between then was a well-defined uptrend.

FIGURE 17.1 Consolidations in a Channel (Google in 2006–2007).

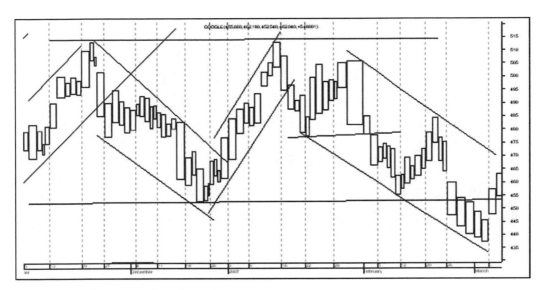

FIGURE 17.2 The Smaller Channels.

Looking more closely, we notice that there are smaller ups, downs, and laterals within that larger pattern. On the second chart of Google (Figure 17.2), we are looking at just a part of the prior chart.

It is also apparent that we could take the smaller swings in the second chart and break them down into component waves in the same manner. All the way from the minute-to-minute ups and downs to the long swings that last for months, stock prices are constantly oscillating. The trend lines help us to define the limits of those oscillations. And by defining the oscillations that make up the trend we are trading, we are able to ascertain if the stock is still acting as we expect it should.

TREND LINES

Trend lines are really no different from support and resistance levels, except that they are reflecting a changing situation rather than a static situation. When the changes tend to have a fairly constant effect, we are able to define the series as a trend. The lines defining channels are an additional help, but the upper line in a downtrend or the lower line in an uptrend are the important ones. If we own a stock and it is in a constant uptrend, we want to recognize when that reliability stops. That termination is signaled by a breaking of the line that is connecting the lows.

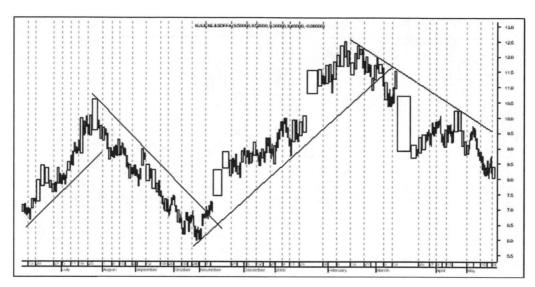

FIGURE 17.3 Uptrend and Downtrend Lines.

On the chart of Kulicke & Soffa (Figure 17.3), each of the major trends is very apparent. Shown are the important lines: the bottom of the uptrends and the top of the downtrends. This stock was so regular we could easily have defined the moves as channels, but doing so would not have helped us in our interpretation. The changes in direction were signaled by the breaking of the trend lines. That is what we need to be watching for.

TREND LINES AND STOPS

When we talked about trailing stop-loss orders, we determined that the best approach was to place stop orders just below each of the ascending lows in an advance or just above each of the descending highs in a decline. Those are the same levels that tend to define our trend lines. But there is a difference. If we are using the stop method, the trend does not have to be as regular, just as long as it continues. The trend line imposes a rigid structure. Look at the chart of Carmax Circuit City in 2006 and 2007 (Figure 17.4).

Often the final move in an advance or a decline involves a steepening and a moving away from the trend line, as in this example. I have inserted the trend line, and also the levels where stops would logically have been entered. Following the stop order regimen would have meant getting out with a somewhat larger profit. But of course the opposite argument can also be made. Sometimes an advance ends with a rounding and slowing rather than a steepening. In that case it would be better to be using a trend line signal, as shown in the example of Kohl's in 2006 (Figure 17.5).

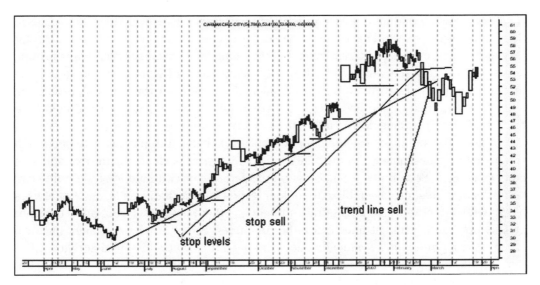

FIGURE 17.4 A Steepening Uptrend.

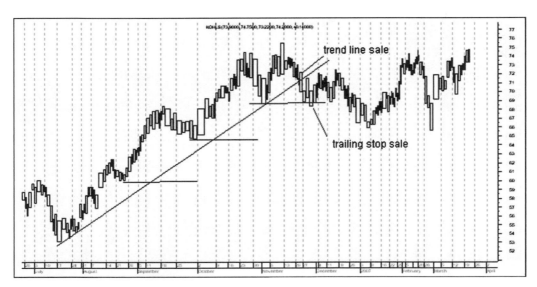

FIGURE 17.5 A Slowing Uptrend.

There is no simple answer as to which method is better. However, there were clues in these two cases. We could have been aware of the accelerated uptrend in Carmax Circuit City and drawn in a steeper trend line, thereby being alerted sooner that it was turning down and trusting the validity of our stop. On the chart of Kohl's, the down volume through the trend line would have been an alert that maybe all was not well, prompting us to be concerned by the breaking of the trend line. It had already warned us on the prior pullback by trading down on unusually heavy volume.

Straight lines tend to be quite effective, because change often appears to occur in a somewhat regular manner. But the trends are not always as perfect as in the examples we have examined. Sometimes trends slow or accelerate, but continue. A straight line can be misleading in such cases. I like to look at trends as just that, trends, and not always require them to conform to an arbitrary straight line that I have inserted. Nature does not usually operate in straight lines, but rather in curves. So, by inserting straight lines we are imposing rigidity on a system that does not need to pay attention to that rigidity. For that reason, I suggest watching the trend and drawing the lines to gain information, but using stop orders, as discussed before, to manage a holding.

CHAPTER 18

Targets

There appears to be a direct correlation between the sideways moves (discussed in Chapter 16) and the trending moves (discussed in Chapter 17). If we look at history, it is apparent that narrow consolidations tend to lead to smaller moves, while wide consolidations lead to longer moves. But it is not a time relationship; it is a volume relationship. It appears that the more stock that is traded in a base, the more stock that is traded in the ensuing advance. And it appears to be a share-to-share relationship. That is, the number of shares accumulated in a base is likely to be about the same as the number of shares distributed in the move that follows.

This makes sense. Stocks go through stages of accumulation, followed by advances, followed by tops, and then by declines. If the general situation in the stock has not greatly changed, then the float stays about the same, and that float goes through stages of accumulation and distribution. The more accumulation, the more selling on the way down. Of course, there can be radical changes in a stock, such as new financing that adds to the supply and therefore to the float, that can throw this off. But generally we can get a good idea of where a move is likely to go—up or down—by the sideways area that precedes it.

MEASURING VOLUME WIDTHS

Because Equivolume charts are being used, we can measure the amount of volume as width on the horizontal axis. A given measurement, let us say two inches of width on the chart, represents a certain number of shares changing hands, regardless of how much time it takes. It might be a couple of weeks or three months, depending on how heavy the volume had been. But the same number of shares changed hands during that two-inch distance. The interesting observation is that the width of the base is usually very similar to the width of the subsequent advance, and the width of the top is usually very nearly the same as the width of the subsequent decline. That does not tell us price, because we do not know if the subsequent advances or declines are going to have steep or gradual slopes. But it does tell us that we can anticipate the end of an advance or a decline to be when the lateral distance has been completed. We often refer to it as running out of volume.

In Xerox we see such a measurement. On the chart of Xerox (Figure 18.1), we see the method of projecting a probable top. At the time of the breakout we look back across the valley and see where the other wall of the consolidation occurred. Then we insert a rectangle, which represents the area of accumulation. In that way, we have a hint as to how much volume is going to be used up in the advance. That determines the length of the horizontal arrow. It is the same length as the width of the accumulation box. Of course, when we put in the arrow we do not have any idea how steep the advance will be, so we do not know how high the price is likely to go. But we do have the knowledge that the advance is likely to terminate about where the arrow ends, in terms of volume.

The technique is the same on the short side, as we see in the chart of Harmonic from 2002 (Figure 18.2).

There was an obvious sign of weakness, a power box to the downside that announced a change in the stock. It was going from a lateral move to a decline. The width of the top could be enclosed in a rectangle that was very wide, suggesting a substantial

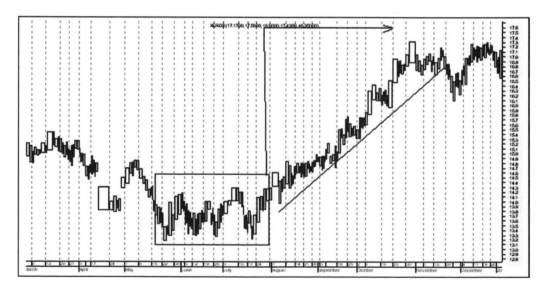

FIGURE 18.1   Projecting a Top.

FIGURE 18.2 Projecting a Bottom.

decline could be in the offing. As the slide progressed the volume was "used up" so that by the time we got to the end of the arrow we could say we had run out of volume, and the decline was probably about over. However, by then we would already have been stopped out if were using our usual trailing stop at each rally high. Also, the downtrend line would have already been penetrated.

In Figure 18.3, we see how such measurements can be applied to the smaller waves also. Accumulation width A is the same width as its arrow. The narrow top, B, leads to a very short decline in terms of volume but not in terms of points lost, because it is steep. Going through the other tops and bottoms, we see a similar relationship between sideways width and slope width.

If we are going to follow each position with a trailing stop order, is there any reason to have a target on a stock—an objective? The answer is yes, for two reasons. The first comes into play before we ever enter a position. We would like to know how far a move is likely to go before we go into the stock because we want the best possible performance. If we see that a stock is likely to go a long way, it becomes more attractive. Given two stocks with similar signs of strength, but one looks as though it could double while the other looks as though it might tack on 10 percent, obviously the one we want to buy is the possible double.

Then, after we own a stock, the idea of a target means that we are going to treat the stock differently. Early in the move we will have more patience, and perhaps give it a little more room with our stops. Later, as it gets close to the objective, we will have far less patience. We will be looking for a reason to take the profit if our objective has been approached, and will be likely to move our stops in closer.

FIGURE 18.3   Step-by-Step Measurements.

I do not suggest, though, that targets be used as a single reason to make a decision. They can be helpful, but they are not accurate enough to be relied on solely. I find that I am often looking at the objective when the advance or decline has lasted quite a while. It can even prompt me to put in a very close profit-taking stop if the stock has used up all its volume. But in that case I am usually also seeing other signs, such as heavier volume in the wrong direction or a breaking of the trend line.

Simply, then, we need to keep our eye on the width of each accumulation or distribution zone as it develops, and project a probable objective when we see a breakout. Then after we have entered a position we will have a chart with a possible target on it. It will serve as a warning when we are getting late in a move, and will also serve to make us more patient early in a move. In addition, if the stock is moving in the expected direction, but the slope of the advance or decline is disappointingly low so that it looks as though we will have only a small profit even if the objective is attained, we may want to become a little more impatient with the stock, either just getting out and moving on or edging a very close profit-taking stop order in.

THE ROLE OF VOLUME

Implicit in the concept of targets is the idea that under these circumstances regular waves will develop that are based on volume rather than time. Especially in the longer term, the number of shares trading upward and then downward tends to be quite regular. That, then, leads to cycles. The cyclicality of a stock is partially based on an underlying cyclicality of the markets, and partially on its own supply and demand situation. But what emerges, often, is a series of very regular waves, in which the crests and troughs are approximately equidistant. This entire concept formed the basis for an earlier book of mine, entitled *Volume Cycles in the Stock Market* (Equis International, 1994). But the validity and usefulness of cyclicality plays a larger part in the longer-term motions of the markets and the individual stocks. For our uses, recognizing the smaller forces that help to create those cycles, the accumulation to distribution targeting discussed earlier, is more important to our pragmatic trading approach. Readers who want to delve deeper into volume cyclicality may want to get hold of that book.

Two other concepts that I first introduced in earlier books do play a part in what we want to achieve here, though, and are discussed in the next chapter. They are Ease of Movement and volume-adjusted moving averages.

CHAPTER 19

Ease of Movement and Volume-Adjusted Moving Averages

In this chapter I want to cover two other helpful tools that you may want to use. The descriptions will be of necessity brief. Each has been the primary focus or a large part of another of my books, published in years past. Therefore, I will direct interested readers to get those books to delve more deeply into each one. But that is not really necessary for what we are trying to accomplish here, which is to present a pragmatic and simple method of trading.

Ease of Movement and volume-adjusted moving averages (MAs) are complex computations. The original books devoted many pages to the derivation and execution of the computations, under the assumption, necessary at that time, that the reader would be doing the difficult calculations and charting. But modern technology has come to our rescue in the years since those books were written. The programs included on the CD-ROM accompanying this book contain those methods and are easy to use. So here in this chapter we will simply review the basis of the methods, and then see how they can be helpful. The assumption is that you either will use a computer program to derive these indicators or will not include them in your decision-making process. With the power of computers at our fingertips, it does not seem logical to go back and learn the tedious calculations and charting techniques necessary to create the charts by hand and then put the time and effort into keeping those charts.

EASE OF MOVEMENT

The first indicator we will look at is called Ease of Movement. It initially appeared in *Volume Cycles in the Stock Market*. Basically, Ease of Movement was designed to

151

quantify the elements that make up an Equivolume chart. It looks at the shape of each box, the direction of price movement of each day's trading, and the amount of price change. These are all calculated and given numerical values that are then combined to arrive at a single number, which we call the Ease of Movement Value (EMV). That number is a plus or minus number indicating whether it is easier for the stock to move up or to move down. The size of the number indicates how easy or hard it is to move. The raw number is too erratic in itself to be useful, but when a moving average is applied it suddenly takes on meaning. Again, this is all done by the computer, so all you need to do is select Ease of Movement as an indicator that you want displayed, and set the moving average parameter you want applied. The value that is used for the default moving average is usually the 13-day, which was my suggestion in the book. It continues to work well.

Figure 19.1 shows the indicator as the line in the upper part of the chart. It is apparent that the line closely follows what is happening in the stock. But being an oscillator, it moves above and below a centerline, even though the stock may have an up or down slope. With an oscillator, the high points or low points of the indicator are usually near comparable levels, so that it is possible to deduce that it is probably at an extreme level. On this example, the three high points of the Ease of Movement are at about the same upward extreme, but the three corresponding highs on the stock are very different from one another. That can be a big advantage at times. Another advantage over just looking at the price is the ability to apply trend lines to the indicator. In this case it would have been

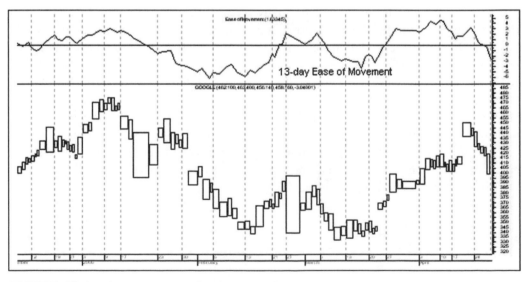

FIGURE 19.1 The 13-Day Ease of Movement Indicator.

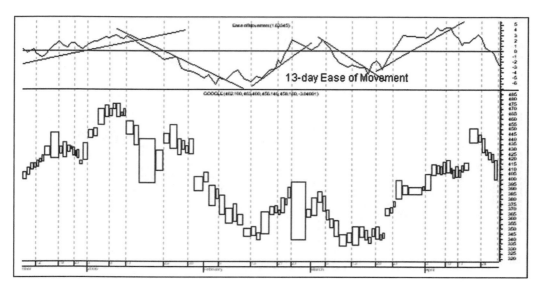

FIGURE 19.2 Ease of Movement Trend Lines.

very difficult to place meaningful and useful trend lines on the price chart because of a few erratic postings. However, the trend lines drop into place quite easily on the Ease of Movement plot, as shown in Figure 19.2. Each time the indicator crossed the trend line it was a valid signal to buy or sell.

Advantages of the Ease of Movement Indicator

An advantage to the Ease of Movement is that even though it is a moving average of an indicator, it does not have the lag time of a moving average of the price. The signals tend to coincide with the turning points, rather than coming in late. For example, look at the chart of Tidewater in 2006 and 2007 (Figure 19.3). Above the chart is the Ease of Movement, with trend lines already inserted. For comparison, a simple 13-day moving average of the price has been placed on the price plot. The moving average does a good job of smoothing the data, but the turns come long after the price has started to reverse.

I suggest using the Ease of Movement as a companion to trend lines as an indication of a possible turning point. If you are long a stock, seeing the Ease of Movement turn down is a warning. There should be a protective stop in there, anyway, but perhaps it could be moved in closer if the Ease of Movement is starting turn over.

Figure 19.4 shows how this early warning from the Ease of Movement saved more of what was only a small profit, anyway. Waiting until the second stop took out the position would have created a small loss, even though the stock did move higher after being bought. Instead, the indicator line started to turn down as the highs were being made.

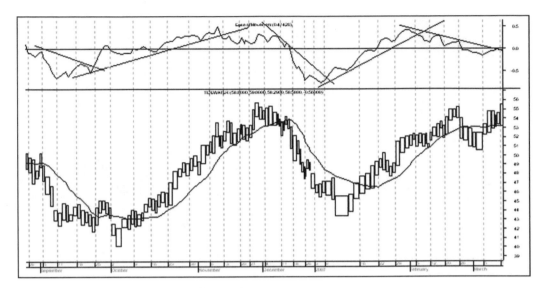

FIGURE 19.3 The Timeliness of Ease of Movement.

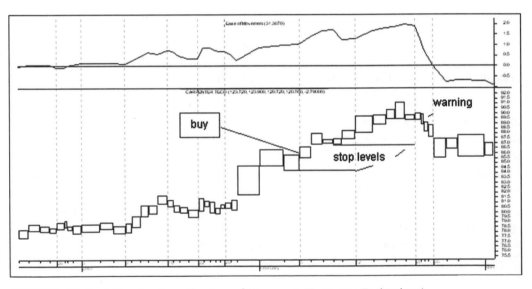

FIGURE 19.4 A Warning from the Ease of Movement (Carpenter Technology).

That suggested the stock was quitting and that the stop should be moved up tighter, thereby preserving a small profit.

VOLUME-ADJUSTED MOVING AVERAGES

The second concept we need to look at in this chapter was not introduced until a later book, entitled *Trading without Fear* (John Wiley & Sons, 1996), where I explained the calculation and charting of volume-adjusted moving averages. As with Ease of Movement, it was a complex calculation that has since been made simple by computers. Now it is no more of a job than electing that the lines be added to the charts and selecting the desired parameters.

The problem with all moving averages is that they contain a lag time, as we saw on the chart of Tidewater (Figure 19.3). The longer the time parameter, the smoother the moving average, but the longer the lag time. The problem is inescapable, even though many methods have been devised to ameliorate it. Exponential moving averages or weighted moving averages just emphasize the more recent data, but even they cannot look into the future to see what the upcoming entries are going to be. Volume adjustment does not avoid the problem, either, but it does a lot to help. The reason is that a volume-adjusted moving average recognizes the fact that all days are not the same. Heavier-volume days are more important than light-volume days. Therefore, they should have a bigger influence in our calculations. Moreover, it is a fact that the heaviest volume tends to come in on tops and bottoms. Those tops and bottoms are what we are intent upon recognizing, so if we give volume a role in the calculation, the tops and bottoms will tend to stand out.

The Volume X-Axis

The idea behind volume-adjusted moving averages is to relate them to the volume-based x-axis, rather than the traditional time-based sequence. To do this, the moving average needs to receive more input from a heavy-volume day than it does from a light-volume day. To simplify a complex chore done by computer, please look at Figure 19.5.

Let us take the narrowest box on our chart and assume it contributes a single piece of information to the moving average, which is its median price for the day. A larger box might be twice as wide, so it would contribute two price entries to the moving average, and a very big day might contribute six entries. Then the moving average is calculated using a set number of volume-based entries rather than a set number of days. In the examples shown, we will be looking at two moving averages on each chart, the 13-volume and the 34-volume. I have found these two parameters to be my favorites. A 13-volume

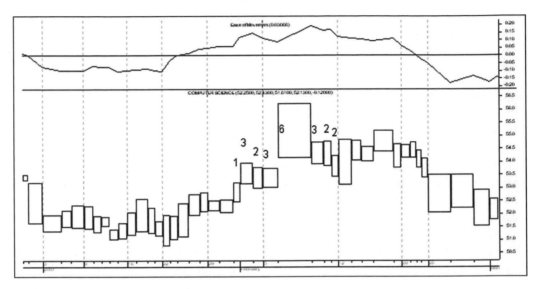

FIGURE 19.5 Variation in Box Widths.

moving average, for instance, is the averaging of the price over the last 13 volume periods, not the last 13 days.

Moving Average Crossovers

It is apparent that the crossovers of the two moving averages in Figure 19.6 are late in this case, but they do tell us when a move is well established. More important here is the change of direction of the 13-volume line. It tends to confirm, very often, what we are seeing in the Ease of Movement line. But on a longer-term basis, the crossovers of the 13 and 34 can be extremely helpful. We see that in Figure 19.7.

From the standpoint of trading, a moving average crossover can be used as an alert to a change of direction, but not as a reason to establish a long or short position. In the first ellipse we see the crossover to the plus side. It is, in this case, a great signal, but so early that it is not supported by any other evidence. But a couple of weeks later the first power box to the upside is seen. That, combined with the crossover, becomes a very compelling signal. On the subsequent top of the advance, the crossover comes in just a few days before the first decline through a higher low. At that point a trailing stop would be executed. I look on the moving averages as confirming or alerting factors rather than demands for action.

I like to display the Ease of Movement across the top of all my charts and the two volume-adjusted moving average lines on top of the price plot as a standard procedure.

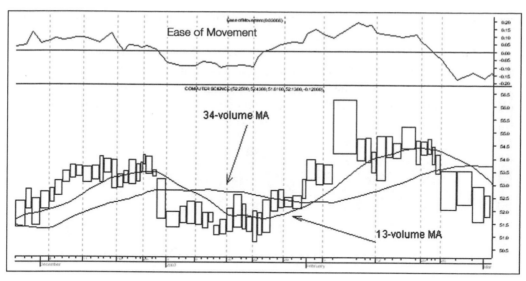

FIGURE 19.6 Volume-Adjusted Moving Average Crossovers.

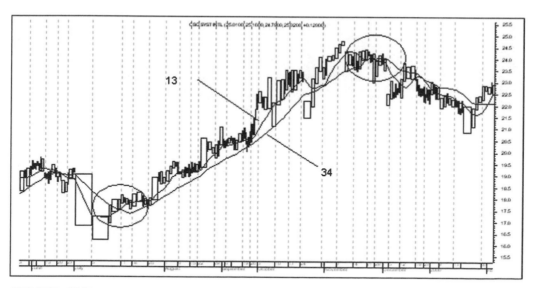

FIGURE 19.7 Crossover Signals (CSG Systems).

Once they have been inserted and defined on one chart, the instructions will carry over to every chart I look at until I change those instructions.

So far we have talked entirely about individual stocks and the decisions we make in trading them. But stocks do not exist in a vacuum. They are a part of the market and are influenced by the swings in the market. It is far easier to make money if one is in tune with the market, rather than fighting it. The next few chapters are devoted to ascertaining what the market is doing and what it is likely to do.

CHAPTER 20

Is the Market Going to Go Up or Down?

That is the question I hear most often. "Is the market going to go up or down?" It is a standard question, put forth to make conversation or to get a little free information. I have a standard answer: "Yes. Yes, the market is going to go up or down." But then I like to go further, so as to not sound flippant and offhand. I like to say that going up and down is exactly what makes the market so fascinating and so profitable. It does go up and down. It does so constantly, and it does so on all levels from the minute-to-minute ripples to the great tides that last many years. And with it the components do the same thing, sometimes in concert with the market and sometimes seemingly in a world all their own. Individual stocks have their rhythms, and so do the industries of which they are a part. Whole segments, like the utilities or the transports, often seem to move together, but even then there are mavericks within the market segment that refuse to conform.

As traders we need to know about those swings and try to go with them rather than fight them. A large component of price movement in individual issues is the effect of market direction. Sure, you can make money going long stocks in a bear market, but it is a lot more difficult than playing the short side in a bear market. Knowing market direction is imperative, I believe.

Many years ago I started to write down, every morning before the market opened, the long-term, intermediate-term, and short-term direction of the market. Not the direction I thought it was going to go, just the direction it was going. I was amazed at the clarity it brought to my thinking. I was not telling the market where it should go, nor where I thought it was going to go. I was merely observing what was happening. I found that there were times when I was buying, yet the market was clearly moving lower. There were other times when I didn't have any stocks or had lightened up on my holdings

159

because I thought the market had gone too far, but the reality was that the market was moving higher in the time frame I was interested in. I was fighting the market and trying to impose my will upon it.

OBSERVING MARKET DIRECTION

The first step in studying market direction and using it to our advantage is not one of prediction. It is merely one of observation. This comes back to our earlier realization that the market is always right. If we lose, it is not because the market acted wrongly; it is because *we* acted wrongly. We did not understand the market or the stock we were dealing with. Sure, the unexpected and the unpredictable could come along and throw us off no matter how well we did our analysis, but that is why we always had stop orders to guard against the unexpected disaster. Part of understanding our stock is to place it in the context of a market and an industry. If the markets are on a tear, and have been for weeks, it does not make much sense to be going short. If all the gold stocks are dropping, it is usually evident. Why buy a gold stock under those circumstances, even if the chart looks good? Whenever possible we want to let the market and the stocks tell us their story. That is the same reasoning as we use in placing stop orders to enter positions, rather than market or limit orders. We want to be in agreement with the price movement rather than try to second-guess a turn.

Later on we are going to see that there are certainly times to be a contrarian. In fact, major turns can be our best opportunities for large profits. But most of the time, markets and individual stocks are in trends rather than turns. It is imperative to be aware of the trends and use them. So, instead of asking, "Is the market going to go up or down?," the first question should be, "What is the market doing right now?"

The question is usually remarkably easy to answer. But it has to be answered in the context of our interests. If we are doing day trading, the market direction on a day-to-day basis is important, but probably the outlook for the next five years does not need to play a big part in our considerations. That is not to say it is meaningless. When the technology stocks turned south in the year 2000, it was a good thing to know, even if you were interested only in short-term plays. The technologies were probably not a good place to be trying to profit on the buy side.

Suppose it is late October of 2004 and you are following the discipline suggested earlier of observing each day the direction of the market. Look at Figure 20.1. Throughout most of the year, the Dow Jones Industrial Average has been confined to a tight trading range. The legs have been very regular, and have each had a duration of about a month. It is quite apparent that the current trend is down in relation to that swing frequency. But there is more to be seen than that. If the pattern is to continue, it looks as though it

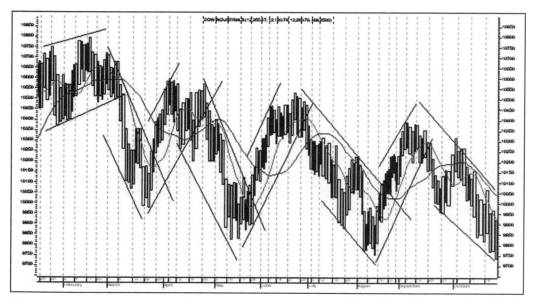

FIGURE 20.1 A Series of Regular Waves.

is just about time for another upswing. But at this time we are only trying to see what the current direction is, and do no forecasting. So we note that the current direction is down.

THE NEXT LARGER WAVE

Now here is the important part. You do not want to observe the direction of the swings you are trading. You want to know the direction of the next larger pattern. So, if you are interested in the swings it is because you are trading within them. In other words, you are going long or short the two or three waves that make up each of the swings we have identified as lasting about a month apiece. So you are making trades that last a few days each, but are looking at the direction of the next larger pattern. If you have identified the next larger pattern as being down, then you will want to use only the short side for your trading. If you have determined that the next larger wave pattern is pointed upward, then you will want to be a buyer of stocks, not a shorter of stocks, until the direction of the next larger wave changes.

The reason for this is, of course, that you will do better if you are trading in the direction of the next larger trend. If it is a downtrend, the down moves will be bigger than the intervening up moves. Trading in the direction of the next larger trend improves the potential return and lessens the risk.

If you are looking at the pattern in Figure 20.1, but are inclined to be buying and selling at the tops and bottoms of the larger swings, then you need to know how what you are looking at fits into the bigger picture. To do that, you need to go out to a longer-term chart, as shown next.

In Figure 20.2, we see that the swings we were looking at before were part of a larger down-sloping pattern (that would tend to be a warning) and that the uptrend that began in March 2003 had turned into a slow slide in early 2004. Shortly after the slide began you should have been aware of it, since the ascending pattern had obviously been broken with the penetration of the ascending lower trend line. It was a shallow enough downslope so that both longs and shorts could have been profitable, but, in theory, it would have been better to concentrate on the shorts rather than the longs, if you had the patience to wait out moves lasting months. In noting the current market direction, we would call it a down market on an intermediate-term basis. But we would also observe that this seemed to be a pullback within a major bull market that began almost two years earlier. So the very long-term picture could still be classified as being up.

As we see in Figure 20.3, the next upswing did materialize just about as we expected, based on the regular cycles, but the move kept on going through the top of the downtrend. It eventually looked like an immense one-year-long flag. From there on the

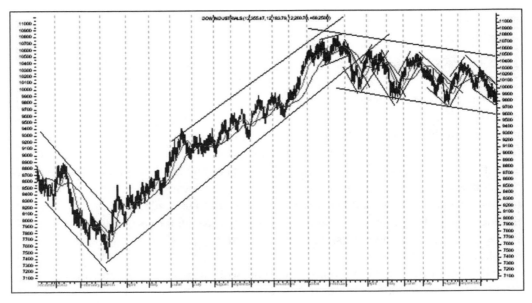

FIGURE 20.2 A Longer-Term Downtrend within a Very Long-Term Uptrend.

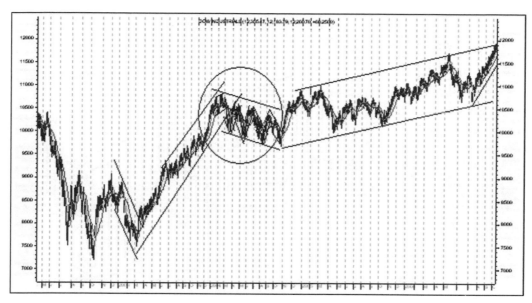

FIGURE 20.3　The Very Long-Term Uptrend Continues.

inclination should have been to primarily use the long side of the market for positions that were trading the big waves.

Broadly, then, we have come to the following conclusions in late October 2004:

- Shorter-term swings, lasting days or weeks: down.
- Intermediate-term trend, lasting weeks or months: down.
- Long-term trend, lasting years: up.

But we also could have moved in the other direction and taken advantage of shorter-lasting, smaller moves. In Figure 20.4, I took a part of the first chart and enlarged it.

Here just one of the previous waves is seen to consist of a number of up and down moves, each lasting just a few days. The trend has been down, but now, at the time of the observation, it looks as though the last wave has gone further than expected and has penetrated the next larger trend line. It is telling us an up move at the next larger level may be starting to materialize. It is suggesting we may want to be trading on the long side, since a reversal in that direction is apparently developing in the next larger wave.

The fractal effect can be followed back to the hourly and even the one-minute charts, in order to determine direction. The intent is the same: to identify the direction of the next larger move as a hint of which side of the market to be trading.

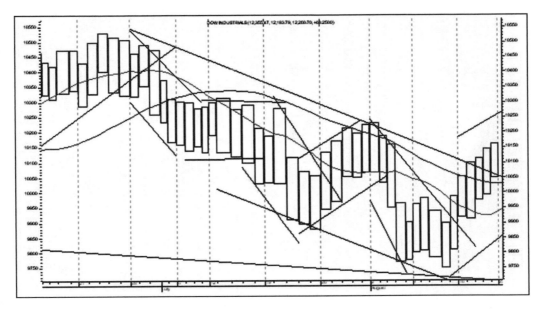

FIGURE 20.4 Close-Up of Two Months.

So, it is not legitimate to ask whether the market is going to go up or down until we first determine what time frame we are referring to, and also until we decide what it is already doing. In this chapter, we have been careful not to mix prediction with observation. Observation needs to come first, but there are also many technical factors that can help us in making predictions. Let's move on to see what the technical picture can tell us about what to anticipate and either take advantage of or guard against.

CHAPTER 21

The Arms Index

I n the preceding chapter we purposely avoided talking about market forecasting. It was decided we needed to first ascertain the current condition of the market for the time frame we were watching. We were acting as observers, not predictors. But forecasting has its place. The problem, though, is that forecasting so often takes on the role of trying to ascertain when a change of direction is likely to occur, whereas trend following is usually more profitable than reversal spotting. That is why we addressed trend determination in the prior chapter. But there are times when we can benefit hugely if we can correctly determine when a change is happening or about to happen.

Wouldn't it be nice to have one single measurement of the markets that would give us a good idea of times when we were approaching an important turning point? It would not have to be telling us every move we wanted to make, but it would need to alert us to the really important levels within the time frame we were trading. There are, of course, a myriad of indicators that purport to do just that. Also there are many technical tools other than indicators that help in determining turning points. In the next chapter we are going to look at some of those technical tools. But with the many indicators available, it is possible to have too many. Unless they all agree, which is unlikely, you are going to be confused. I want to show you just one in this chapter that I believe is all you are going to need. Any other observations may help to solidify the belief you have garnered from this primary indicator. Do not overload yourself with indicators.

All we really want to do is determine when it is getting very late in an advance or a decline, because it is at that time that we may want to change our emphasis. If we are in a long advancing move, but we observe that we are getting overbought, we may want to start emphasizing holding more cash or adding some shorts in anticipation of a downturn. But, remember, if we are following our discipline of letting stop orders get us in and out, we are not going to look at an indicator and decide to sell everything and go short. Instead we may want to move our stops in closer, and we may want to look for potential shorts so that a reversal will touch off stop orders that initiate such positions. If we stick with the belief that it is better to not argue with the market, but let it tell us its story, then we will not be premature in our moves by anticipating a turn that does not occur.

One of the possible drawbacks to using a single indicator is that it might quit working. That has happened to indicators in the past, usually because they became too popular. As more and more people started to use them, they tried to anticipate a little earlier than the next guy. As that went on, the indicator became so anticipatory that it failed. That cannot happen to the indicator we are about to study. It is based on the internal dynamics of the marketplace. And those internal dynamics are expressed as price movement and volume. Therefore, no matter how popular it may become, the index is self-adjusting. The people who act upon it create volume and price movement, so the index, rather than being hurt, is just reflecting that very action. This index has been around for about 40 years and has a huge following. In those years many analysts have tried to write its obituary, but it continues to be effective. Even the writers of the obituaries are contributing to the data that the index reflects.

The Arms Index started its life being called the Short Term Trading Index, because that was how I first presented it in an article in *Barron's*. Later, one of the data providers abbreviated that title to TRIN. Another data provider called it MKDS. It was only years later that it started to be called the Arms Index. But these and various other abbreviations used by data providers all refer to the same simple calculation, which we will call, of course, the Arms Index.

THE CALCULATION

The calculation of the index is very simple. It compares the ratio of advances to declines to the ratio of advancing volume to declining volume. It is designed to ascertain whether the stocks that are rising are receiving less or more than their fair share of the volume. Here is the formula:

$$\text{Arms Index} = \frac{\text{Advances/Declines}}{\text{Advancing Volume/Declining Volume}}$$

At any given time we can ascertain the four necessary pieces of information. Ever since 1967 the figures have been available for the number of stocks on the New York Stock Exchange that are higher for the day and the number of stocks that are lower for the day. If it is during the day, the numbers represent the condition so far for the day, which will change constantly. We ignore the stocks that are unchanged. Similarly, the volume traded on those stocks is calculated during the trading day, so that we have a number that shows the total number of shares traded on the advancing stocks and another for the total number of shares traded on the declining stocks. Plugging those four numbers into the formula, we derive the Arms Index for the instant when it is calculated.

AN EXAMPLE

Let's look at an example. On a recent trading day, about two hours into the session, there were 1,030 stocks up for the day and there were 2,036 stocks showing losses for the day. So, by dividing 1,030 by 2,036 we come up with ratio for that part of our calculation of 0.5058. At the same time there had been traded, so far that day, 160,308,000 shares on the stocks that were up and 359,783,000 shares on the stocks that were down. Dividing those numbers, we come up with an advancing volume to declining volume ratio of 0.4456. By then dividing the first ratio by the second we arrive at the Arms Index for that instant, which comes out to 1.14. Any number over 1.00 indicates that the declining stocks are receiving more than their expected share of the volume, and any number under 1.00 says they are receiving less than their expected share of the volume. In other words, over 1.00 is bearish and under 1.00 is bullish. In this case, the down stocks are getting a bit more volume than they should, indicating selling pressure.

Usually the index is likely to be somewhere between a bullish reading of .60 or so and a bearish reading of 1.60 or so on a typical trading day. There are, of course, extreme days when we see the index as low as .30 or as high as 10.00 or more. But the very big numbers are rare, with only one huge panic-type number every 10 years or so. Usually if we are seeing a very low number it is telling us that an inordinate amount of volume is flowing to the buy side of the market. It is a bullish indication for that instant, but, as we will see, it can combine with other such readings to say that things are getting too bullish, and probably the advance is unsustainable. Similarly, a number over 2.00 during the trading day is telling us that the down stocks are getting twice their fair share of the volume, and it indicates fearful dumping of stocks. Often that fear can become overdone, leading to a buying opportunity.

The interpretation and use of the index are wide-ranging and beyond the scope of this chapter. There are variations in the calculation, and every conceivable moving average has been applied to it over the years. For those who want to delve more deeply into the subject, I have written an entire book entitled *The Arms Index* (Marketplace Books, 1996). But, for our purposes here, we will look at the simplest, and probably still the best, methods of applying the index—the various simple moving averages using a few selected time periods that seem to be the most useful for aggressive traders.

MOVING AVERAGES

The construction of a moving average is a simple process, but it is especially handy when a computer program can do it for us. The first moving average we will look at is a five-day moving average. In other words, each day the values for the prior five closes of the index are averaged and posted. That produces a line on the chart that we can then relate to the level of the market.

In Figure 21.1, the lower black line is the five-day moving average of the Arms Index. It is compared to the Dow Industrials over a seven-month period in 2005. From now on, let's refer to the index itself as the Arms Index, but the moving averages of the index will be abbreviated as AI, so this is the five-day AI. It is immediately apparent that the peaks on the AI relate very closely to the low points in the Dow Industrials. Moreover, all the troughs in the AI point directly to minor tops in the market.

Three horizontal lines have been superimposed on the AI chart to make it easier to see how levels relate to one another. The centerline is 1.00, or neutral for the index, and will not vary. The other two lines are arbitrary. We have used 1.30 and .85 because they represent extremes in the context of this particular time period. But they would not necessarily be pertinent in another type of market; this happened to be during a quite flat market. Do not ever try to impose hard-and-fast exact levels for overbought and oversold conditions on any of the time frames we will be studying. Look for extremes compared

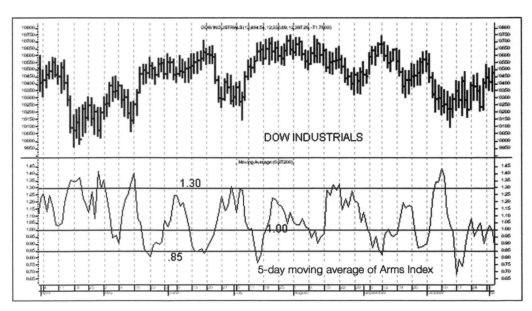

FIGURE 21.1   Five-Day Moving Average of the Arms Index.

to recent history. It will always be somewhat of a judgment call, but all we really want to do is find out if we seem to be in a danger zone.

MAKING THE CHARTS MORE MEANINGFUL

There are two changes I like to make to these charts. The nature of the AI is such that peaks and troughs are counter to the peaks and troughs in the market. Therefore, I like to invert the scale for the AI. With a computer program it requires nothing more than checking a box to do so. In addition, the Arms Index calculation gives us a number that can be infinitely large but cannot go below zero. That means the distance above 1.00 gets bigger much more easily than the distance below 1.00 becomes smaller. To correct that is also a simple task; I change the vertical scale to a log scale. See Figure 21.2 for an example.

If your trading orientation is very short-term and aggressive, the five-day AI is going to be very useful to you. You know that every time it gets to a level quite far from that centerline it is becoming overdone. When that happens, there could be a little lag time, perhaps a day or two at most, and then the market is extremely likely to be turning in the other direction for a few days. The AI is telling you that on a short-term basis the market has been too bullish or too bearish for too long. They are small extremes, but they are tradable.

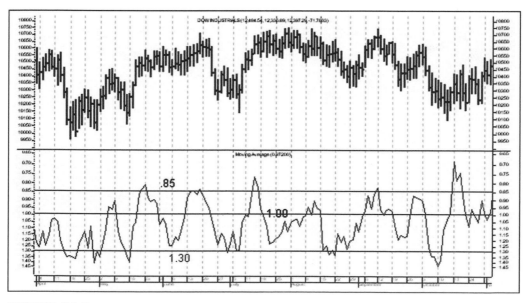

FIGURE 21.2 Inverted Log Scale.

The next larger scale is the one that seems to get the most attention on Wall Street. Perhaps that is because it is a scale that was so often relied upon in the days before computers made all calculations easy. It is the 10-day AI. The 10-day AI is looking at much more important market swings than was the five-day. The five-day is a great short-term trading tool, but the 10-day can give us warnings of impending changes in direction of much larger importance. Figure 21.3 shows us the 10-day AI over a two-year period, centered on the market bottom in 2003.

This chart shows us a number of things. First, notice the coincidence of tops and bottoms in the AI to tops and bottoms in the market averages. They occur much less often but are much more meaningful than what we were looking at in the five-day. They catch important tops and bottoms that could be very costly if ignored. But also notice that they are not as uniform in the levels of their extremes. We know that steep advances toward the top of the chart are warning of a market turndown waiting in the wings, but the exact level is not reliable. That is particularly true of the spike upward in October 2003, which was right after a major low. That is typical when coming off an extreme oversold condition, and it is something that needs to be anticipated. But, in general, the peaks and bottoms are good signals of overdone conditions.

But now look at the vertical line that has been inserted to differentiate between the bear market that began in 2000 and ended in 2003 and the bull market that followed. It is apparent that the warning parameters changed at that time. In a bear market the whole

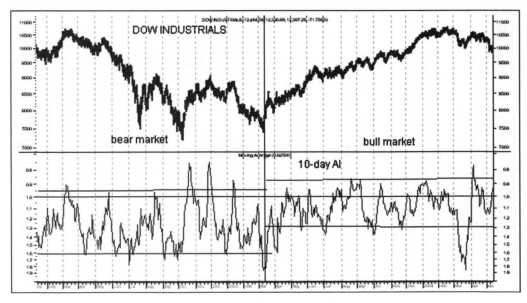

FIGURE 21.3 The 10-Day Moving Average of the Arms Index.

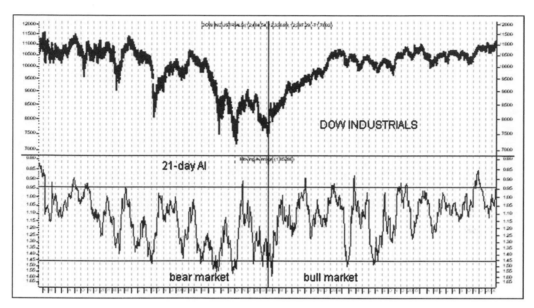

FIGURE 21.4 The 21-Day Moving Average of the Arms Index.

scale tends to move toward more bearish levels. This points out the need to be aware that no numerical levels are absolute. What we need to do is look for extremes and use them as warnings.

The moving average that is most important if you are trading for the larger swings is the 21-day AI. This moving average is extremely accurate and should never be ignored. It is longer-term, and picks out only the major highs and lows. Moreover, it tends to be more uniform in its levels. As we can see in Figure 21.4, there is little distinction between the bull and bear markets that played a large part in the levels of the 10-day AI.

With these three moving averages, we have covered the levels that are applicable to our aims. The AI is an indication of where we are and what we may be able to expect. A downward plunge of the AI is a strong indication of a bottom about to be made, reflecting indiscriminate dumping of stock over a period of time. People are panicking, and when there is panic selling we need to be thinking about going the other way and buying, rather than being carried away by the emotions of the crowd. Orderly advances and declines are times when we want to be conformists, but when emotions get out of hand we want to be contrarians. There are times when it pays to go against the direction of the rushing masses. The AI is very helpful in recognizing those times, because it is measuring the internal buying and selling pressures of the marketplace.

CHAPTER 22

Market Tops and Bottoms

As we noted in Chapters 20 and 21, in order to make logical decisions we need to identify the current direction of the market, rather than try to second-guess turns. But there are certainly times when recognizing a turn a little ahead of time, or as it is taking place, can be a wonderful opportunity. The trick is knowing when to be a follower and when to be a contrarian. The Arms Index can be a big help in recognizing those extremes, as can the structure of the market itself.

Look at Figure 22.1. Markets run through a cycle that starts with panic, evolves into cautious buying, then displays increasing confidence. That is followed by universal confidence and complacency. When the complacency is seemingly well entrenched, some cracks in the structure may start to appear. There are unexpected sell-offs that produce lower lows rather than higher lows. The next stage is increasing concern and fear as prices start to slide. Soon fear becomes prevalent, then universal, leading eventually to panic selling. Then the cycle starts again.

In this scenario we want to be aware of where we are in the cycle at all times. Under most of those conditions it is fine to go with the crowd. In fact, it can be disastrous at those times to think we are smarter than the crowd and oppose the move. If investors are starting to become mildly more confident, they will push prices higher; when they are becoming concerned, they will drive prices lower. Even in the later stages of the up or down legs, it can be costly to say that the crowd is wrong and go against them, while recognizing the extremes of fear or greed can be very profitable.

The usual analogy for the action of the stock market is a comparison to a roller coaster. And certainly the thrills, the laughs and screams, the fear, and the exhilaration are all there. The analogy ends there, though. The path traveled by a roller coaster is

173

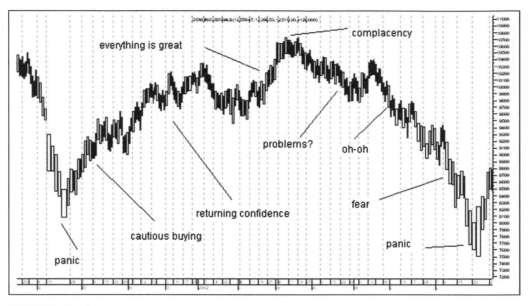

FIGURE 22.1 The Market Cycle.

quite different from that of the stock market. A roller coaster climbs up long hills and then sweeps through rounded and twisting valleys, before roaring up the next hill. The tops of the market are much like those of a roller coaster, but the bottoms are very different. They are more like the bottom of a deep crevasse; there is seldom a nice rounded structure that gradually changes a downward plunge into a new rise. If we are looking for an analogy, the pattern traced out by the stock market, and less so by individual stocks, is like the path traced by a boy on a pogo stick. He rises to a smoothly slowing arc at the top of the pattern, and then drops to a sharp and abrupt shocking bounce off the ground. The upward path is one of deceleration to a turning; the downward move is one of acceleration, so that the maximum speed and force are seen just before the bounce.

POGO STICK BOTTOMS

When we combine volume with price movement in the Equivolume method, the pogo stick analogy is particularly noticeable, because we are more aware of the amount of energy involved in each part of the cycle. (See Figure 22.2.)

Recognizing the bottom of a decline is usually amazingly easy in retrospect, but at the time it is sometimes hard to believe it is happening. Rudyard Kipling's "If you can keep your head when all about you are losing theirs . . ." comes into play here. Panic is so easily

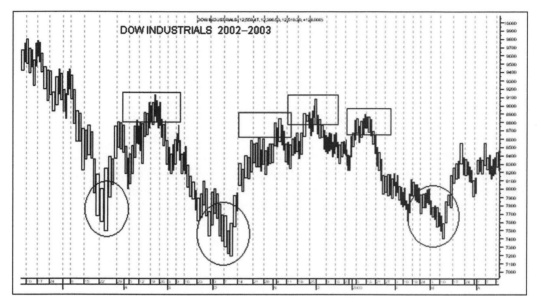

FIGURE 22.2 Pogo Stick Market.

transmitted that only a very disciplined person can resist it and take advantage of the situation. But there are clues for the person who remains clearheaded. Both the volume and the trading range expand dramatically as the low is being made. On an Equivolume chart these clues show up as very tall and wide boxes. Such action is depicted in the areas enclosed in ellipses in Figure 22.2.

The real clue that it is time to buy is a day with a wide trading range, or two consecutive days with wide trading ranges, in which a sudden reversal is seen. The one-day reversal often consists of heavy selling through much of the session and then a powerful advance toward the close, so that the price finishes the day at or very near the top of its trading range. In the two-day scenario, the first day is down and the second day is up, with a close near the high. This is such a common way to end a decline that it is usually unmistakable when it happens. It is just like the bounce of the pogo stick.

MARKET TOPS

Market tops are not as easily identified. That is because, like the ride on the pogo stick, there is a slowing and a turning rather than a dramatic occurrence. Usually there is not one dramatic incident that announces a top is forming. There are, nevertheless, hints that show up on the charts. Unlike a bottom, a top is typified by narrower trading ranges.

Volume does get heavy, but the trading range tends to lessen rather than expand. The result is often a series of short and wide Equivolume boxes, all in a tight trading range. Such action is telling us there is a barricade to further progress, stretched across the chart just above the current price. Every time the price tries to get through it, volume expands as it uses up a great deal of effort, but the level is unbreached. It is like a goal line stand in a football game. Referring back to Figure 22.1, we see such a consolidation in the area labeled as complacency. In Figure 22.2, each of the top areas is enclosed in a rectangle. All of them exhibit this tendency to stall with heavy volume.

Of course, the various indicators we have looked at can also be applied. In Figure 22.3 we see the Dow Jones Industrial Average in the second half of 2006 and into 2007. The Ease of Movement is displayed across the top, and has had trend lines inserted. The two volume-adjusted moving average lines are the 13-volume and the 34-volume. Often with a market average, the daily is too close a look. We are interested in getting an idea of the longer-term trends within which we are trading, so it is often worthwhile to stand back and get a more general picture. I like to change to a weekly chart, but still keep the same parameters for the moving averages.

Figure 22.4 shows a weekly picture of the Dow, which includes the data from the prior chart. On this chart the two moving average lines give very clear and unequivocal signals. It is also more apparent on this chart rather than the daily chart that volume

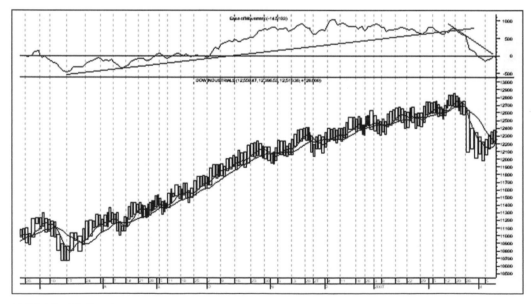

FIGURE 22.3   Short-Term View.

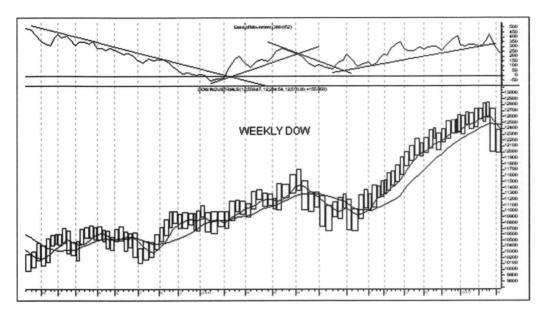

FIGURE 22.4 Longer-Term Look.

was getting heavy but the trading range was tight as the market made the final high. It encountered very difficult resistance, which led to the subsequent rapid and steep break.

By knowing the market direction and being alert for changes in that direction, it is possible to swing the odds further in our favor. To reiterate, before we predict we need to just observe current conditions. In most cases that is sufficient, since markets spend a great deal more time in trends than they do in reversals. Nevertheless, we always want to be alert to possible changes of direction, without succumbing to the temptation to second-guess the turns. Often the turn does not come nearly as soon as we think it is going to. We may eventually be right, but we may get hurt in the meantime. Never should we put ourselves in the position of arguing with the market, because *the market is always right.*

CHAPTER 23

In Conclusion

When you step into the stock market and lay your money on the bar, you are not unlike the white-hatted cowboy in the B western movie who steps out of the hot, dusty sunshine of the frontier town and into the dark, smoky, crowded saloon.

"Howdy, stranger," says a mean-looking black-hatted gunslinger at the bar. All heads turn toward the door to size you up. There is not one customer there who has any desire to help you. You are an adversary—someone whose defeat could show them a profit. Taking you out can add another notch to a gunslinger's reputation. There is little apparent respect even if you have a big six-shooter hanging low on your gun belt. They all have six-shooters. Perhaps you can outdraw most of them, but the chances are that at least one of them has a faster draw than you do. And there are a lot of them who can work together against you.

You have a choice to make. You can belly up to the bar, toss down your money, and order a whiskey, as you confront the row of desperados who are lined up with one foot on the rail, one hand holding their whisky and the other close to their guns. Or you can walk slowly into the saloon, nod, smile, and find a quiet table with your back against the wall, where you can quietly watch the room. After a bit of observation, the crowd may decide to ignore you, and you can size them up, mentally separating the good ones from the bad ones.

Becoming a gunslinger sounds glamorous and exciting, but it can also get you killed. When you are looking for trouble, you are sure to find trouble. And as the stranger in the crowd, the odds are certainly not in your favor. Nevertheless, as a gunslinger you are going to have a lot of excitement, and, if you survive, you will have a lot of successes to brag about. You may eventually be the one to stand at the bar and say "Howdy, stranger" to the next wannabe to walk into the saloon. But the odds are better that you will be buried at sunset.

By comparison, being an observer and going with the flow sounds dull, but it is a lot safer. It means surviving longer and having time to learn. It means remaining inconspicuous, seated at a quiet table and drinking alone. There is nobody to brag to. But having the wall at your back and watching the crowd works. If a gunfight is imminent, the patrons who do not want to get shot or get in the fight retreat to the street. That is when you are going to go with the crowd. But if a panic breaks out and everyone is trampling each other rushing for the door at the same time, that is when you are going to want to step up to the bar and calmly order another whiskey.

In the stock market, the safety wall at our back is the stop-loss order we place. It precludes anyone sneaking behind us and shooting us when we are not watching. It allows us to relax and observe, without being carried away by fear. We know that wall is there, without having to turn around and check on it. That leads to logical rather than emotional decisions. We can sit back and observe all the characters in the saloon, deciding which ones could be our friends and allies, and which ones to avoid.

Once we have identified a possible friend we can act friendly toward that person, but we want to wait until he or she decides to come our way and act friendly also. In other words, we want to go with the flow of the friendship, rather than trying to turn an enemy into a friend. In stocks that is what we are doing if we buy a stock that is going down or short a stock that is going up; we are trying to force a reversal. It is better to buy a stock when it is already doing what we want it to do and expect it to continue to do. Using stops to enter positions does just that.

If a fundamental analyst, a quantitative analyst, and a technician were all sitting at quiet tables, looking at the row of desperados at the bar and wondering which to take on, the fundamental analyst would need to know the ancestry of each candidate, the brand of gun he was carrying, and the type of bullets he was using. It might help to know the name of the horse he rode in on and the outfit he was wrangling for.

The quantitative analyst would be interested in knowing the draw time of each candidate. He would want to ascertain his wounded-to-killed ratio and his hit-to-miss ratio. It would be important to ascertain whether the candidate shot better in summer or in winter, and whether rainy days affected his performance.

The technician would want to know which gunslingers were drunk and which ones were not. He would want to know if one was a loudmouth braggart, or another a surly drinker. He would watch to see who seemed to be spoiling for a fight and whether any of the gunslingers were part of a group who acted together. He would be more interested in current conditions than it past history.

As technicians (or psychohistorians) we are going to be the quiet cowboys waiting for opportunities. We are going to always protect our backs and never start a fight. We are going to go with the crowd until it becomes a lynch mob. But we are going to always be watching for the times when the mob loses all reason, and never go with them at that point. We will never brag about the notches on the butt of our gun, but we will amass them as the opportunities present themselves. And we will be the survivors and the winners.

About the CD-ROM

INTRODUCTION

This appendix provides you with information on the contents of the CD that accompanies this book. For the latest and greatest information, please refer to the ReadMe file located at the root of the CD.

SYSTEM REQUIREMENTS

Operating System	Windows Vista, XP (Service Pack 1 or higher), or 2000 (SP 4 or higher)
Processor	Minimum: 800 megahertz (MHz) processor Recommended: 1 GHz or faster processor
RAM	Minimum: 256MB Recommended: 512MB or higher
Video	Minimum: Video card and monitor supporting at least 256 colors at 1024 × 768 Recommended: Video card and monitor supporting at least 32-bit color at 1024 × 768 or higher
Hard Disk	Minimum: 300MB available space Recommended: 800MB or greater available space (for system testing)
Internet Connection	Minimum: 56k Internet connection Recommended: High-speed Internet connection
Other	Mouse or other pointing device CD-ROM drive Internet Explorer version 6.0 or later with the latest service packs MAPI-compliant e-mail program

USING THE CD WITH WINDOWS

To install the items from the CD to your hard drive, follow these steps:

1. Insert the CD into your computer's CD-ROM drive.
2. The CD-ROM should start to install automatically.
3. You will be asked for a setup key. Use the following number: KK7E-GRVQ-U4M7J
4. With the CD you receive the first month of data free of charge to use with the program. To activate the data feed, go to www.metastock.com/arms.
5. Once you have completed the sign-up at www.metastock.com/arms, you will receive your user ID and password for the software from Equis International via e-mail.

   If the opening screen of the CD-ROM does not appear automatically, follow these steps to access the CD:

1. Click the Start button on the left end of the taskbar and then choose Run from the menu that pops up.
2. In the dialog box that appears, type *d:***start.exe**. (If your CD-ROM drive is not drive *d*, fill in the appropriate letter in place of *d*.) This brings up the CD interface described in the preceding set of steps.

WHAT'S ON THE CD

This CD-ROM contains a free 30-day subscription to MetaStock End-of-Day. MetaStock End-of-Day is specifically designed for traders who do their analysis after the markets close. Whether you're an experienced, active trader or just learning how to trade the markets, MetaStock helps you succeed. The software contains powerful analysis tools to help you make informed decisions about what to buy and sell and when to execute to make the most money possible. MetaStock comes with many out-of-the-box trading solutions that are reliable and easy to use. And if you want to take your analysis to the next level, MetaStock gives you the ability to customize these solutions to your particular trading style.

   The charts are set up for you to mirror the charts in the book. This way you can apply the chart settings directly and apply the strategies learned from the book.

CUSTOMER CARE

If you have trouble with the CD-ROM, please call the Wiley Product Technical Support phone number at (800) 762-2974. Outside the United States, call 1(317) 572-3994. You can also contact Wiley Product Technical Support at **http://support.wiley.com**. John Wiley & Sons will provide technical support only for installation and other general quality control items. For technical support on the applications themselves, consult the program's vendor or author.

To place additional orders or to request information about other Wiley products, please call (877) 762-2974.

For technical support on MetaStock, please call Equis International at (801) 265-9998 or e-mail support@equis.com. To activate the data feed, please go to www.metastock .com/arms.

Customer Note: If This Book Is Accompanied By Software, Please Read the Following Before Opening the Package

This software contains files to help you utilize the models described in the accompanying book. By opening the package, you are agreeing to be bound by the following agreement:

This software product is protected by copyright and all rights are reserved by the author, John Wiley & Sons, Inc., or their licensors. You are licensed to use this software on a single computer. Copying the software to another medium or format for use on a single computer does not violate the U.S. Copyright Law. Copying the software for any other purpose is a violation of the U.S. Copyright Law.

This software product is sold as is without warranty of any kind, either express or implied, including but not limited to the implied warranty of merchantability and fitness for a particular purpose. Neither Wiley nor its dealers or distributors assumes any liability for any alleged or actual damages arising from the use of or the inability to use this software. (Some states do not allow the exclusion of implied warranties, so the exclusion may not apply to you.)

Index